Sounding Prose

Quiringh Gerritsz. van Brekelenkam, *Interior with a Lace-Worker and a Visitor*, 1650–68 (detail). Oil on panel. Rijksmuseum Amsterdam SK-A-673.

Sounding Prose

Music in the 17th-Century Dutch Novel

Natascha Veldhorst

ANTHEM PRESS

Anthem Press
An imprint of Wimbledon Publishing Company
www.anthempress.com

This edition first published in UK and USA 2022
by ANTHEM PRESS
75–76 Blackfriars Road, London SE1 8HA, UK
or PO Box 9779, London SW19 7ZG, UK
and
244 Madison Ave #116, New York, NY 10016, USA

British Library Cataloguing-in-Publication Data
A catalogue record for this book is available from the British Library.

Library of Congress Control Number: 2021953402

ISBN-13: 978-1-83998-300-9 (Pbk)
ISBN-10: 1-83998-300-0 (Pbk)

Cover image: Gesina ter Borch, *Man Reading to a Woman*, 1660–61.

This title is also available as an e-book.

CONTENTS

FIGURES

ACKNOWLEDGEMENTS

This work was supported by a grant from the Netherlands Institute for Advanced Study in the Humanities and Social Sciences (NIAS). I am very grateful for this fellowship that provided me with invaluable research time and the privilege to be part of an inspiring intellectual community. This essay has benefited from the discussions and feedback at the NIAS. Many thanks to Hans Luijten and Eddy de Jongh for their fortuitous comments on previous drafts of the text. I am also indebted to my anonymous Anthem peer readers, who generously shared their knowledge and ideas. Moreover, I am thankful to Huigen Leeflang for his help with the illustrations, and to Patrick Grant and Bart Westerweel for their meticulous linguistic advices.

1

INTRODUCTION

A while ago, my attention was drawn to a term that I came across in a newspaper. I remembered seeing this term first in a discussion of Jennifer Egan's novel *A Visit from the Goon Squad* (2010). Shortly thereafter, I saw it again in a review of Erik Menkveld's *Het grote zwijgen* (2011), a novel featuring two Dutch composers, Matthijs Vermeulen and Alphons Diepenbrock. Since then, I have encountered it more often, and it has now come into common usage amongst literature reviewers. The term is 'music novel'.

Music novel: it sounds so obvious – a novel that is partly or entirely about music. Everyone has read one: classics, such as *Doktor Faustus* (1947) by Thomas Mann or *De koperen tuin* (1950) by the Dutch author Simon Vestdijk, or more recent examples, such as Nick Hornby's *High Fidelity* (1995), Vikram Seth's *An Equal Music* (1999), *Het psalmenoproer* (2006) by Maarten 't Hart, or *Swing Time* (2016) by Zadie Smith. Websites and printed bibliographies present lists of the titles of hundreds of such music novels, as if the usefulness of such information were self-evident.[1] Upon closer inspection, however, the term is remarkable, given the lack of similar descriptive words for novels in which other art disciplines are prominently featured. Why is it that we never talk about theatre novels, literature novels, dance novels or visual art novels?

Music unquestionably has a special relationship with literature. The two disciplines have always been closely linked, and the connections between them have been discussed for centuries. In recent decades, these have also been the subject of in-depth, systematic examination within the academic field known as 'musico-literary studies', also known as Word and Music Studies, which is part of the broader area of research on 'intermediality'.[2]

In musico-literary studies, researchers pay attention to a broad range of connections between the disciplines and across a wide variety of literary and musical genres, including song, opera, poetry and prose. Musical influences on the novel vary wildly. Music can play a role in many different ways, and the purpose of a musico-literary analysis is to highlight these diverse elements, in order to say more about the content, structure and expressiveness of the literary work as a whole.

Such research has generated a much better idea of what music means for literature. It shows, for example, that the influence of music is not limited to poetry, which still tends to be the first thing people think of whenever the relationship between the two art forms is mentioned. Its influence can be seen in prose as well. Within prose, music can emerge as a theme, either one-dimensional or multilayered, as in Tolstoy's *Kreutzer Sonata* (1889), in which Beethoven's famous violin sonata drives the characters to madness and, eventually, to murder. Music can also influence the structure of the novel, as is the case in the famous 'Siren chapter' in *Ulysses* (1904), which James Joyce claimed was written as a *fuga per canonem*, and in Toni Morrison's *Jazz* (1992), a novel characterised by an associative jazz-like writing style borrowed from the music itself, or in *The Waves* (1931) by Virginia Woolf, in which music plays a role at all levels, determining both the form and style of the book.[3] As Gerry Smith notes in his book *Music in Contemporary British Fiction*, with regard to English literature:

> Music looms surprisingly large in the history of British fiction. Novelists from every generation, working within every genre, have responded to the power of music, by trying to harness its techniques and effects, and by attempting to recreate the emotions that come to be associated with particular musical styles, forms or texts. In fact, music represents a recurring feature of the canon – one ranging from those texts in which it plays a seemingly incidental (although usually strategically significant) role to those in which it permeates the formal and conceptual fabric of the literary text.[4]

The late 19th and early 20th centuries bear witness to the enormous wealth, variety and experimental efforts in this area. Many writers of this period express their explicit debt to music. In the preceding era of 19th-century romanticism, the status of music had changed. No longer seen as subordinate to literature as it had been before,[5] music enjoyed a greater prestige and was labelled the 'most romantic art' (as described by the German author, critic and composer E. T. A. Hoffmann). Consequently, music was held to be best suited to expressing the romantic ideal of 'the sublime'. In other words, what was once considered a handicap – the absence of narrative – was now seen as a strength. It was evident to the romantics that music had the capacity to express the essence of human existence without words and without images, precisely because it lacked a narrative. Faced with new opportunities and prospects, artists from other disciplines began to focus on the characteristics of music for their own work. Music became a pre-eminent model. As the English critic and author Walter Pater wrote in 1888, 'All art constantly aspires to the condition

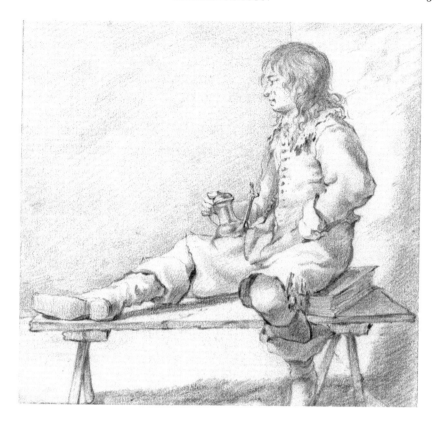

Figure 1. Constantijn Verhout, *Young Man Seated on a Book*, ca. 1650–ca. 1660. Black chalk. Framing lines in black chalk and brown ink. Rijksmuseum Amsterdam RP-T-1967-92.

of music.' Inspired by the special qualities of music, writers – as well as artists, sculptors and architects – crossed the boundaries of their own disciplines, thus opening them up for innovative experiments.

Musical influences can be found in the work of nearly all the major writers in the years around 1900. For both poetry and prose, music apparently offered new possibilities that would permanently change literature. It is not surprising, therefore, that a substantial body of musico-literary research has focused on this period. This, of course, also applied to the study of music novels that concentrated especially on the turn of the century, later expanding to include the entire 19th and 20th centuries.[6] In this context, it is important to note that some scholars deliberately do not use the term 'music novel'. In their view, the word is overly suggestive and misleading: how much music should a book contain in order to be labelled as a music novel, and in what ways should music feature in such a work – as a subject, as a means of fleshing out the characters or, at least, as a structuring principle? Some novels that include music could hardly be described as music novels, because music does not serve as the main theme. The dividing line is difficult to find and determine. In short, while the term 'music novel' is frequently used by reviewers and critics, I prefer to speak of 'music in the novel', as has already been done elsewhere.[7] A more neutral description like this makes it possible to determine the degree to which music is present, and then conduct a systematic analysis of the significance of the role of music in the novel.

2

MUSIC IN THE NOVEL BEFORE 1900

In recent years, I have often lectured on literary developments in the years around 1900, and my focus was always on the crucial 'shift towards music' and on the century that followed, with musical authors including Milan Kundera, Thomas Mann, Simon Vestdijk, Jack Kerouac and Toni Morrison.[1] This material by itself is enough for a lifetime of study, but gradually I found myself attending more and more to the presence of music in earlier novels. The 17th century was of particular interest, primarily due to recent publications noting that the novel had flourished to an exceptional degree during that century: hundreds of prose texts were printed, both in the Netherlands and abroad, and people loved them. However, a second reason for my curiosity had to do with the musicality of the 17th century. I have previously addressed the relationship between music and literature during that century in both a monograph on the use of music and songs in the Amsterdam theatre, and in a study about the popularity of songbooks in the Netherlands.[2] Therefore, I was well aware of the ubiquity of music and song in that era, in the arts as well as in people's daily lives. At that time, music was at least as pervasive in Dutch society as it is now. Combining all these considerations, I started wondering about the situation preceding that of the new prestige accorded to music in 19th-century literature. In particular, I was interested in the 17th century, when authors were producing an abundance of prose fiction as well and were obviously also inserting music into their texts.

Samples from 17th-century Dutch prose indicate that this incorporation of music was indeed extensive. Moreover, musical elements were also present in the novels of other European countries. A search in the academic literature on the subject did not, however, yield much detailed information. Compared to the 19th and 20th centuries, there is very little research on musical influences on literary prose from earlier times. Here, the prevalence of poetry apparently still stands.[3] This neglect is also due to the fact that prose is often connected to the 'transformation of the oral into the literary'.[4] In surveys of the development of the novel, either national or international, there is virtually no attention to the subject. In fact, my research has revealed only a single side note in a survey study, in addition to a handful of articles, a

Figure 2. Jan Lievens (attributed to), *Young Woman Reading*, undated (17th century). Etching. Rijksmuseum Amsterdam RP-P-OB-762.

chapter and two books.[5] And yet, already in 1972 Esther Garke drew attention to the subject in an introductory essay on *The Use of Songs in Elizabethan Prose Fiction*, in which she stated that even though 'scholars have started to discuss the use of songs in drama, the corresponding study of the use of song in prose has hitherto been neglected'.[6] Since then, the situation has remained virtually unchanged. Even in a canonical, exhaustively studied novel such as Cervantes's *Don Quixote of La Mancha* from 1605 (considered by some to be the first European novel), the musical aspect has been largely overlooked. In a 2013 article on the subject, the American hispanologist Chad M. Gasta observes that, even though 51 of the 126 chapters in the book contain songs and/or musical references, 'the topic has received scant attention'.[7] In his

Figure 3. Simon Guillain (II), after Annibale Carracci, *Bookseller*, 1646. Etching. Rijksmuseum Amsterdam RP-P-2015-26-926.

study *Music in the Georgian Novel* from 2015 Pierre Dubois also points at the lacuna, first in general: 'Surprising as it may seem, there is at present no book offering a global survey of this question [...]. Whereas the presentation of music in romantic poetry has been studied, there is to my knowledge no equivalent for prose fiction.' Subsequently he notes with regard to eighteenth-century British fiction: 'The study of music in the Georgian novel has been strangely neglected, either because it is considered to be of only circumstantial importance in the narratives in question, or because it is thought to be a "specialist" interest and hence below the notice of the serious literary critic.'[8] The same goes for the Netherlands: so far, no studies whatsoever have been conducted on the role and function of music in early modern Dutch prose fiction.[9]

In the course of my research, I became increasingly intrigued by the subject. I would have liked to have studied the entire range of 17th-century European novels, in order to subject them collectively to a musical analysis. This is a daunting task, however. The novel was a widespread European phenomenon in those days. Translation and exchange took place on a large scale, and books travelled rapidly across borders. Certain works were published in five or six languages, and subsequently influenced national traditions. Some were so successful that they were reprinted more than thirty times.[10] The world is witnessing 'a deluge of novels', the Italian writer Vicenzo Nolfi complained in 1646, in the preface to his 'anti-novel' *Elena Restituita*: 'Honestly, the current century is going mad with the writing and reading of novels.'[11] Prose fiction was successful not only in quantity but also in quality. In *Seventeenth-Century Fiction* (2016), the French literary historian Isabelle Moreau observes an 'astonishing variety of fictional experiments at the time'.[12] The popularity of the novel was international and many of the texts were interlinked beyond national borders. That is why it would be worthwhile to read and study everything. However, the inclusion of all European sources would be a formidable task, and for this reason I shall concentrate on the Dutch repertoire: a challenge that is sufficiently demanding and complex in itself, especially given the fact that in order to deal with it effectively it is necessary to take the international context into account.[13]

3

PROBLEMS STUDYING THE EARLY MODERN NOVEL

As has been pointed out many times, 'novel' is a problematic term, especially for this period, because many texts are quite different from what is currently regarded as a novel. They are frequently fragmented in structure, lack a coherent plot and do not offer genuine character development. Basically, they are sadly lacking, according to modern standards. This 'uncontrolled' element explains why the texts look rather like hybrids to us, from the point of view of the genre as we now understand it. For that matter, even more than at present, the prose of the 17th century was immensely varied. The texts are highly diverse in scope, content and form. It might therefore be better to use the umbrella term 'prose fiction', as is usually done in medieval and early modern studies, instead of referring to 'the novel', which quickly and unintentionally generates modern expectations and connotations. Nevertheless, for the sake of stylistic variety (and also, bearing in mind John Frow's observation, from his lucid exploration of *Genre* (2015), that 'genres have no essence, they have historically changing use values'), I will occasionally use the word 'novel', alternated with other options like 'prose' and 'prose texts' that are considered as synonyms here.[1]

Another problem, and one that makes research on music in 17th-century prose fiction rather difficult, is the fact that, to date, no surveys have been conducted on the genre in the Netherlands. This omission has already been observed in 2002 by the literary historian Inger Leemans, and little has changed since then.[2] In other countries the study of the early modern prose fiction has moved forward substantially in recent years, both in the European and national perspectives.[3] For the Netherlands, however, scholarly treatment of the repertoire has been limited to a number of interesting sub-studies and some articles devoted to individual texts. Scholars of Dutch literature treat the novel differently and significantly less extensively than is the case for the drama and poetry from the same period. That is the reason why there is no overarching, summary study of the repertoire. Dutch researchers are aware of this gap, even referring to the prose fiction of this period as being 'the

Figure 4. Ferdinand Bol (attributed to), *Seated Old Man with a Book*, undated (17th century). Etching. Rijksmuseum Amsterdam RP-P-BI-2001B.

odd man out' in the field of literary history.[4] It is nevertheless unclear why this is the case. Why has the genre been so academically undervalued in the Netherlands?

The reasons underlying the relative neglect of the 17th-century novel in Dutch literary research are diverse. First, prose fiction was not highly valued at the time, and even long thereafter. Contemporaries do not seem to have considered prose texts very 'literary'. At the same time, this was precisely the reason why some authors chose to adopt this specific style of writing. For example, we know that Johan de Brune the Elder's primary reason for deliberately choosing to write prose was that he didn't think of it as a literary medium. For him, content was more important than form, and unadorned prose was thus ideal. The absence of rhetorical flourishes and forced rhymes made prose suitable for conveying the message as directly as possible: 'The same goes for eloquence as for water: it's best if it is pure and light and has hardly any flavour. It is a subtle art not to use art' – an unmistakable reference to Ovid's well-known statement, *Ars est celare artem* ('It is art to conceal art').[5] Apparently, it was also the conviction of the French author Jean Puget de la Serre, who praised his own prose as follows: 'The style is neutral and natural; the phrasing is clear and evident. In short, what makes this art is precisely the fact that it is devoid of it.'[6]

In literary terms, but also in a moral sense, 17th-century prose fiction was not held in high regard. The genre was frequently denounced at the time, and the many fashionable novels and novellas were regarded as lewd, superficial and trite. In the Netherlands and elsewhere, critics pointed out the 'corrupting effect of so much fiction' and 'the waste of time involved in such a trivial pursuit'. Such criticism nevertheless failed to detract from the popularity of the genre, which flourished.[7] Three centuries later, researchers were still complaining about the questionable value and the woefully low literary quality of prose fiction. In his *Ontwikkelingsgang der Nederlandsche letterkunde* (1924), the literary historian Jan te Winkel counted Samuel van Hoogstraten's novel *Haegaenveld* (1669) amongst 'the most curious creations that unchecked imagination has been able to produce'.[8] In *Romans in proza* (1899), his colleague, Jan ten Brink, referred to Baltes Boekholt's *De wonderlijke vryagien* (1668) as 'an excruciatingly bad work'.[9] The opinion expressed on the same text by the literature historian Eddy Grootes in 2004 essentially amounted to the same: 'Of course, in modern eyes, it's just pulp literature.' The criterion of quality continues to echo here. At the same time, however, Grootes found Boekholt's work interesting in historical terms, 'mainly because it certainly had success in its own time'.[10]

In studies on the subject, the literary quality of 17th-century prose fiction is measured by two main standards. First is the contemporary standard, which usually finds expression in negative assessments based on the fact that the texts do not meet contemporary expectations. The second, international standard, argues that the texts cannot compete with contemporaneous foreign examples and at best are poor imitations. In this respect, Leemans rightly argues for greater attention to the specific Dutch character of the novel at the time.[11]

It is not my intention at this point to present concrete examples of high-quality prose fiction in order to contradict the negative judgments. I would nevertheless like to take a moment to reflect on the fact that the early, negative verdicts have continued to weigh so heavily that an entire genre has remained virtually unstudied in our national literature. From the 17th century alone, hundreds of texts have been handed down. It is highly unlikely that all of these texts are worthless from a literary perspective, especially given their popularity at the time. Something else must be at play.

The novels themselves do not appear to be the problem: the issue lies with us. We are the ones who have difficulty with the episodic structure of the texts, whereas this apparently did not pose any problem at all to the readers of the 17th century. To us, the infamous 'sausage-link structure' is confusing rather than entertaining and engaging.[12] We read the random connections and strange accumulation of unlikely encounters, extraordinary phenomena, enigmatic events and insane adventures with some degree of puzzlement. We see only chaos and fragmentation. But why, in the first place, are we so eagerly searching for coherence and cohesion? Despite all our personal efforts, as well as the entire existing body of literary-historical research, we apparently cannot let go of our modern demands and expectations. And that's exactly what it takes. A more open approach is required, because these texts are different from what we expect, and they must be read in a way that can be traced back to a different *use* of texts.[13] As observed in 2006 by the literary historian Johan Koppenol, 'The required reading approach for a 17th-century novel is completely different than for a modern one'.[14] Prose fiction of the time was intended not just to be read in silence and seclusion but also to be read aloud in company. In the latter case, people did not consume an entire book all at once, but instead only in small portions, with each reading being a clearly defined episode (thus, to some extent comparable to the consumption of today's Netflix series or, for instance, that of the popular 19th-century serial novel, by Charles Dickens and others), so that one book was good for several sessions. In this way, it fulfilled a crucial function in social life and it was tailored to a collective, oral context. This insight has already been formulated for the 17th-century Dutch novel, but it has yet to be the subject of serious exploration.[15]

One might find inspiration in the work that has been done by scholars in English literature over the past few years. In *Voices and Books in the English Renaissance* (2019) Jennifer Richards states that the attention to the material object of the book and an overemphasis on silent reading have hampered our view of books as tools for oral communication. 'Today it is acknowledged that oral reading was common, but the idea it should lie at the heart of the history of Renaissance reading has still not been taken up,' she writes and concludes the book by asserting that 'the voice is currently a niche area of study'.[16] In *The Matter of Song in Early Modern England* (2019) Katherine

Figure 5. Jan Luyken, *Pieter Bekjen Reading to a Company in a Boat on the River Amstel*, 1685. Etching. Rijksmuseum Amsterdam RP-P-OB-44.290.

Larson also championed the need for a performance-based analysis of early modern literature: 'Unpacking the performance-oriented facets of texts whose connection to music and song may be obscured for 21st-century readers has much to tell us about the aural processes of reading and reception practices in the period.'[17] Prior to this, Christopher Marsh had already drawn attention to, what he aptly called, 'the sound of print' in the early modern period: texts were 'things that flew through the air, vibrating eardrums as they went'.[18]

A similar exploration was undertaken by researchers in the field of medieval studies some decades earlier. For example, in her study *Orality and Performance in Early French Romance* (1999), the American literary historian Evelyn Birge Vitz calls for 'a fundamental revision of the history of early French romance', believing that 'oral and performed traditions were far more important in the development of romance than scholars have recognised'.[19] In 2005, she and her colleagues championed what would come to be known as 'performative reading' in a number of later publications:[20] 'Just as we keep performance potential in mind when reading Shakespeare's plays, we should do so when reading medieval stories. Analysis of performance is essential for understanding and appreciating medieval narratives because they are

Figure 6. Rembrandt van Rijn, *Woman Reading*, 1634. Etching. Rijksmuseum Amsterdam. RP-P-OB-737.

intended for performance. Thinking in terms of performability, moreover, can give present-day readers a sense of the artistry and vitality of medieval narratives.'[21]

It is also interesting to see how 20th-century writers such as Virginia Woolf and Milan Kundera ingeniously incorporate music and other non-standard elements into their own novels. In their essays they praise the special freedom and playfulness of the early modern novel. In early prose fiction the requirement of probability did not apply, the story or plot was not seen as the most important component, and the extemporaneous aspects of oral presentation remain evident in the format of the text.[22] Kundera points out that early novels should not be judged by later standards.[23] Woolf praises Philip Sidney's *The Countess of Pembroke's Arcadia* (1590) as an inexhaustible literary source: 'In the Arcadia, as in some luminous globe, all the seeds of English fiction lie latent. We can trace infinite possibilities, it may take any one of many different directions.'[24] By extension, in *The Lives of the Novel* (2003) the literary theorist Thomas Pavel regards early prose fiction as 'living literature rather than ossified historical evidence [...] to recapture their appeal'.[25] He also states that 'the early period should not be seen as mere preparation for a genuine rise of the novel in the 18th century'.[26] Pavel further notes that 'one reason why the novel's early development was not always properly understood is that for so long there were no written rules meant to govern prose narrative'.[27] Unlike drama, epic and poetry, prose has been subject to hardly any regulation since antiquity, partly due to the fact that, in contrast to these other forms, the genre had not been discussed by Aristotle.[28]

In no other literary genre a writer had so much freedom. Almost everything was permissible, from mixing conventions from different narrative traditions – pastoral, novella, romance, picaresque – to inserting existing and new stories, anecdotes, poems, letters and songs, as well as including fragments of non-fiction. It is precisely the combination of these different types of texts within a single containing form that must have been attractive to readers at the time. In 1991, the literary historians Jelle Koopmans and Paul Verhuyck referred to this as '*Gattungsvielfalt*: the open possibility of incorporating many characteristics as a characteristic in itself'.[29] They used the definition in their study of anecdote collections, but the description is equally applicable to prose fiction. According to Koopmans and Verhuyck, today's discomfort is due to current classification systems rather than to a lack of a sense of taxonomy on the part of our ancestors. The literature of the 17th century is characterised by 'allusions to other literary conventions to an extent that invites us to wonder whether such interferences, rather than being disruptive elements in our classifications, do not belong to the core characteristics of a literature that is not founded on classical and Aristotelian regulations'. With regard to the Dutch situation, they note that the 'existence of such a plurality within historical literature has not yet been specifically investigated and all too often seems to be excluded in advance'.[30]

The novel, then, is the ultimate open literary form. It is not surprising that other terms have been used to characterise the genre such as 'hybridisation' and 'montage technique'.[31] The novel's hybridity can be especially attributed to the aforementioned episodic structure, in which loose narrative parts were welded together in a seemingly random manner, as well as to the unbridled incorporation of other genres, both literary and non-literary.

4

MUSIC AS AN INSERTED GENRE

Before addressing the musical aspects of 17th-century Dutch prose fiction (i.e. the 'novels' of the time), I would like to devote some attention to the phenomenon of 'inserted genres' mentioned before. While studying the texts, I came across many musical references and songs, as well as many examples of other integrated genres. The regular prose sections in the novels are very often interspersed with poetry, prints and alternative prose elements such as sayings and letters, all of which share with music the fact that their presence and function in the novel have been the subject of little or no specific investigation.

In surveys of the novel and monographs on its history, the topic of inserted genres is usually not treated separately – neither with regard to individual examples nor in a general sense. One exception is the work of the Russian philosopher and literary critic Mikhail Bakhtin, who introduced the term 'incorporated genres' (or 'inserted genres') in a wide-ranging essay from 1934 to 1935, *Discourse in the Novel*, which is the final part of *The Dialogic Imagination*, his collection of four essays on the novel. Bakhtin regarded the phenomenon as an essential characteristic of the novel, a typical feature of the genre throughout the ages, noting its ubiquity: 'The novel permits the incorporation of various genres, both artistic (inserted short stories, lyrical songs, poems, dramatic scenes, etc.) and extra-artistic (everyday, rhetorical, scholarly, religious genres and others). In principle, any genre could be included in the construction of the novel, and in fact it's difficult to find any genres that have not at some point been incorporated.'[1] He distinguished between 'artistic' and 'extra-artistic' genres, and also between existing (externally integrated) and new genres (invented by the writer). Moreover, his concept of 'dialogism' is illuminating in the context of such insertions, for it helps to explain the connections between different types of language combined in a single work by discovering the relationship among the various parts of a hybrid work.

In addition to Bakhtin's notion of 'incorporated genres', the much older term 'prosimetrum' has been used for centuries to denote texts consisting of a combination of poetry and prose. The word itself, a contraction of *prosa* ('oratio' or 'straightforward speech': text without poetic ornament) and *metrum* (verse),

dates back to the Middle Ages. The earliest mention can be found in Hugo of
Bologna's *Rationes dictandi* (early 12th century), which described the phenomenon as 'the mixed form' (*mixtum*).[2] Prosimetrum texts are known from classical
antiquity, the Middle Ages and the Romantic period. Some scholars also regard
contemporary novels, such as Vladimir Nabokov's *Pale Fire* (1962), as examples.

In any case, the insertion of music and songs into 17th-century prose
fiction should clearly be studied within this broader context. My analysis will
be limited to Bakhtin's 'artistic genres'. In the corpus of prose texts that I have
examined, this specific category is very common. 17th-century 'artistic genres'
in prose involve both existing and new elements, including letters, sayings,
dramatic dialogues, illustrations and poetry. Poems (both Dutch and French)
are carved into trees,[3] they are pulled out of gentlemen's pockets and they are
frequently quoted or sung by the characters. Research on this use of poetry in
prose texts is fragmented and has received no detailed attention until now. At
most, comments amounted to little more than a few surprised observations
following the examination of individual texts. 'Poetry interrupts the prose,'
notes Grootes in his article on Boekholt's *De wonderlijke vryagien*. Although he
finds this remarkable, he is even more surprised by the novel's non-fictional
element – an 'extra-artistic' extension that he sees as a 'Fremdkörper'.[4] This
view is shared by the literary historian Andreas Solbach. In his review of
the 17th-century German novel on Martin Opitz's *Schaefferey von der Nimfen
Hercinie* (1630) – modelled on Sannazaro's 1504 *Arcadia* (the pastoral text
that, like Sidney's *Arcadia* from 1590, alternates constantly between prose and
poetry) – he remarks: '*Hercinie* and subsequent works in the tradition of the
prose eclogue do not fit well into the category of the novel – because it mixes
prose and verse freely.'[5] Ernst Robert Curtius is also critical of the practice in
his survey of the various combined forms that can be found in medieval Latin
literature: 'It is characteristic of the Middle Ages' unformulated but living
feeling for art, that writers are fond of uniting and crossing these stylistic
devices [...]. All these minglings and transitional forms testify to the same
taste. They betray a childish delight in play and variegated color.'[6] Mixing up
things is, in other words, not conducive to enhancing the quality of literature.
Therefore, in the view of many researchers, poems, songs, letters and non-
fictional elements do not really belong in the novel.

In my research, I also came across many inserted letters, and they frequently occur in heroic gallant novels modelled after the French style. These
texts often involve several intertwined tales of love, making it necessary for the
yearning lovers to write to each other constantly. These inserted letters are an
example of what Gustave Flaubert would later refer to as 'le réel écrit': that
is, they provide an excellent opportunity for showing the inner life of the
characters.[7] Readers have the feeling that they are not reading literature, but

instead material taken directly from life. There is then a suggestion of natural authenticity, of a sometimes 'raw' reality, permeating the fictional world. Although the epistolary novels of the 18th and 19th centuries have been thoroughly studied, hardly any research on the phenomenon of inserted letters in historical prose texts has yet been done.

Figure 7. Image of a musical scene (serenade) in *Dordrechtsche Arcadia*, a novel by Lambert van den Bos, 1663, between pp. 364–65. Engraving. Koninklijke Bibliotheek, National Library of the Netherlands. 2108 E 21.

Illustrations are used throughout the 17th century in a variety of prose texts. Extensive attention has been paid to this phenomenon in prose fiction of later periods (e.g. with regard to imagery in fairy tales, gothic novels and pornographic novels), but visual aspects of the 17th-century novel have received only scant attention. The few examples include a study of Honoré d'Urfé's *L'Astrée* – the highly popular 17th-century novel that has been embellished with numerous illustrations over time – which demonstrates the shift that occurred in the function of illustrations in the course of the 17th century: from merely visual and theatrical support of the text to an independent means of affecting the reader. 'Le langage de l'image [...] semble être devenu non plus celui de la parole et de la théâtralité mais celui de la rêverie et de la sensualité.'[8] Of course, prints made the texts more attractive to the public from the outset. For the Netherlands, it is worthwhile to compare illustrations in novels with those that were included in printed stage plays. It seems that certain musical scenes (e.g. the serenade) were visually popular in both theatre and literature.

To my knowledge, not much attention has been paid to the mixing of genres by the prose writers of the 17th century, which they probably considered as a matter of course. Nevertheless, the few times that it is mentioned do indeed confirm that blending literary forms was seen as a common practice. For example, in his *Gründliche Anleitung zur Teutschen accuraten Reim- und Dicht-Kunst* (1704), the German writer Magnus Daniel Omeis argued for 'allerhand Neben-Gedichte und Erweiterungen' in the novel, such as 'zierliche Person-Ort- und Zeit-Beschreibungen, lange Unterredungen, Sermocinationes, erbauliche Lehr- und Lob-Sprüche, schickliche Gleichniße, Schlachten, Ludos Circenses & Comicos, annehmliche Carmina, Liebes- und andere Briefe'.[9] A similar recommendation had previously appeared in Sigmund von Birken's *Teutsche Rede-, Bind- und Dichtkunst* (1679), the first theoretical treatise on the novel in Germany (originally published in 1669 as a preface to Anton Ulrich's novel *Aramena*), in which 'die Mänge und Mängung der Geschichten, und deren Wieder-Entwickelung' was emphatically mentioned as a goal which required the blending and interweaving of stories, both fiction and non-fiction.[10] I have not yet been able to find any Dutch statements on the matter. There is a quotation, however, in the preface to Pierre-Daniel Huet's popular treatise, *Traité de l'origine des romans* (1670), which was published in Dutch as *Verhandeling van den oorspronk der romans* (1679). The translator, G. van Broekhuizen, pointed out that no such text about the novel had ever appeared in the Netherlands before and that Huet's treatise was the first of its kind. At first glance, Huet seemed to take a contrary standpoint, writing, 'What are called novels are actually fictions of love entanglements that have been written in artful prose for the education and amusement of readers.'[11] This

Figure 8. Cornelis Visscher (II), *Seated Woman with a Book in her Lap*, ca. 1654–ca. 1658. Black chalk, with stumping, on vellum. Framing line in black chalk or graphite. Rijksmuseum Amsterdam. RP-T-1898-A-3685.

definition aims to make a distinction between the new novels in prose and the old ones from the Middle Ages, which could consist of verse as well. Think, by way of example, of the large 12th-century poem *Roman de la Rose* by Jean Renart versus the vast prose romance *Le Roman de Tristan en Prose* from the same era (both examples include in fact many inserted songs, and also make extensive use of letters).[12] The main characteristic that the two types of the old and the new novel have in common is the fictional element. Huet adds that the new 17th-century novel 'must be written according to certain rules, otherwise they would be muddled, disorderly, and without any charm'.[13] Is his text an argument against the mixing of genres? No, because in the same breath he advances Honoré d'Urfé's *L'Astrée* as a worthy example. *L'Astrée* is a French novel cycle in which the prose is loaded with poems, songs, letters and illustrations.[14]

Another plea for 'incorporated genres', from a much later date, can be found in Friedrich Schlegel's *Brief über den Roman* (1800):

> Ich kann mir einen Roman kaum anders denken, als gemischt aus Erzählung, Gesang und andern Formen. Anders hat Cervantes nie gedichtet, und selbst der sonst so prosaische Boccaccio schmückt seine Sammlung mit einer Einfassung von Liedern. Gibt es einen Roman in dem dies nicht stattfindet und nicht stattfinden kann, so liegt es nur in der Individualität des Werks, nicht im Charakter der Gattung.[15]

Schlegel had put this ideal into practice shortly before, in his novel *Lucinde. Bekenntnissen eines Ungeschickten* (1799), a whimsical prose work full of poetic fragments and inserted letters.[16]

Throughout the ages, from the 12th to the 19th century, numerous writers included songs in their prose fiction: Giovanni Boccaccio, Miguel de Cervantes, Honoré d'Urfé, Friedrich Schlegel and many others. It would therefore only be natural to assume that this practice applied to 17th-century novelists in the Netherlands as well. In the following paragraphs, I examine the question of whether, and if so, when, how and why, the Dutch writers of that time integrated songs and other musical elements into their prose fiction.

5

MUSIC IN 17TH-CENTURY DUTCH PROSE FICTION

Before embarking on my present project, I had no idea in which prose texts I could expect to find music. I therefore decided to keep the corpus as broad as possible at the start, and to compile a list of all prose fiction texts between 1600 and 1700.[1] In doing so, I did not distinguish between translated and original works and included all Dutch-language fiction of the period. In total, this amounted to some three hundred titles.[2] I then studied about a hundred of these titles from the period between 1600 and 1650, plus a few examples from the second half of the century. I searched these texts for the presence of musical terms, while also making a note of lyrics and melody indications.[3] Obviously it would be ideal to do this also for the material from the second half of the century. However, my initial selection already provides a number of important insights.

While reading, I kept in mind the question of whether the use of music was ultimately the same as what I knew from the literature of later periods. In other words, would the analytic model that Werner Wolf had designed in 1999 be useful for the examination of the lyrics and other musical elements in these earlier prose texts, or would it take on a completely different role and function?[4] And in the latter case, how could the differences be best described?

I will start by reporting some practical results. I have identified five main categories in the Dutch prose of the 17th century.[5] In approximately one-third of the texts, music plays no role at all (1).[6] In about a quarter of them, music serves as a theme, that is, it is discussed by the narrator or by the characters in one way or another (2). In one-fifth of the texts, music serves as a theme, and song texts are also included (3). One-sixth of the texts has music as a theme, as well as song lyrics, and indications of the corresponding melodies (4). Music notation is very rare in these novels. I found only two examples (5).

Although this classification might be of some use in itself, it becomes much more interesting when it is brought to bear on the development of the literary use of music. Prose texts without any reference to music (1) and texts in which music plays a thematic role (2) occur throughout the 17th century. The same applies to prose in which lyrics are included (3). However, it is interesting to note that the number of texts from this latter category increased considerably after the 1630s. This was apparently due to the influence of new foreign successes, including *L'Astrée* by Honoré d'Urfé, the great French pastoral novel cycle from 1607 to 1627 which was translated into Dutch, as from 1634. Parts were translated at first, and then, in 1644, the book was published as a single volume. The songs in most of the novels are usually printed in italics, in contrast to the prose text which is in Roman type. In some cases, the strophes of the songs are also numbered.

It is remarkable to see that the lyrics contained in these foreign examples are usually presented 'as poetry' in the Dutch translations. This applies to the translations of D'Urfé's *L'Astrée*, as well as to those of Cervantes's *Don Quixote* from 1657. The translators therefore did not seem to care about the original French and Spanish melodies associated with the lyrics, nor did they try to reinforce or emphasise that these passages were songs, for example, by suggesting their own native melodies (i.e. tunes that were well known at that time in the Netherlands). Two exceptions in which this was in fact done were published and translated by Felix van Sambix in 1643: *Den Ialoersen Carrizale* (*El celoso extremeño*) and *De doorluchtighe dienst-maegt* (*La illustre fregona*), both taken from the *Novelas Ejemplares* (1613) by Cervantes. The first novella contained a *villancico*, a common poetic and musical form in Spain, consisting of four lines:

> Madre, la mi madre,
> Guardas me ponéis,
> Que si yo no me guardo,
> No me guardaréis.[7]

The Dutch translation also contains one song. Van Sambix did not translate the original lyrics literally, however. Instead, he made use of an Italian melody that was popular in the Netherlands at that time – 'Bellissima Mirtilla' – and wrote a new text to it, with a different strophic structure because of the chosen melody. This also resulted in a slight alteration of the content:

> Oh, Mother, what possesses you
> To lock me up like this?
> Why am I being guarded so,
> Tell me what that means.
> What's the point of latch or lock,
> It is ridiculous.
> Alas, alas.
> Love does not want to be

Painfully restrained like this.
Those who love want to be free.[8]

Further research reveals that Van Sambix did not use the original Spanish text as a source, but the French translation of 1614–15 by François de Rosset and Vital d'Audiguier.[9] This version also contains one song with two verses, and its lyrics clearly served as an example for the Dutch version.[10] Unlike the Dutch translation, however, the French one does not have any indication of the tune. The same is the case for Cervantes's other novella, *La illustre fregona*. This work contains five songs. The Dutch translation includes two (both with melody indications), and the French translation includes three (all without tune indications).[11] In this case, Van Sambix used an Italian melody ('Si tanto gratiosa') as well and, this time, also a French one ('O que le ciel est contraire de ma vie'). All in all, this remains somewhat curious, as it is unclear why the translator would include Italian and French music in a Spanish text. Searching for a suitable Spanish melody was clearly not an option for the translators – a 'Southern quality' was apparently sufficient. The most important aspects were the fame and recognisability of the music, and not its origin, textual authenticity or applicability and/or relevance.

Van Sambix embraced what had become a new trend in prose fiction in the Netherlands: the addition of melody indications to the songs (4). Although this was not done by every prose author, it became more common in the 1640s. The trend was started by Jacob van Heemskerck, in his *Inleydinghe tot het ontwerp van een Batavische Arcadia* (1637), a text that is often considered to be the first Dutch novel.[12] It is also seen as the starting point of a mini-tradition of arcadias, in which historical and geographical information is woven through the fictional prose.[13] Van Heemskerck's text contains six songs, five of which are provided with a melody. Such melody indications can be found both in original Dutch novels and in translations of foreign prose texts, although they occur most abundantly in the first category (at least according to my preliminary investigation). Examples include Haring van Harinxma's *Doolhof van Socia* (1643), Gysbert de Sille's *Dwalende liefde* (1645) and Samuel van Hoogstraten's *Schone Rooseliin* (1650). Jacob Heerman's translation of Vital d'Audiguier's *Lysander en Caliste* (1658) contains several tune indications as well, in contrast to the French original. A further interesting example of this Dutch musical quirk can be found in Van Harinxma's translation *Seven wonderlijcke ghesichten* (1641), after Quevedo's *Sueños y discursos* (1627). The translator took the liberty of adding a joke to the original text:

Once they come to execute this plan, we will slam the door in front of them, and when they come to see us, we will sing to them the French song

of Montélimar: to the melody of *Blijf buiten, doortrapte schurken*, otherwise
the devil would be with the calves much sooner than with the cows.[14]

Van Harinxma added the phrase 'to the melody of *Blijf buiten, doortrapte
schurken*', a tune indication that he made up himself (at least I was unable to
find it anywhere else and the meaning of the sentence, 'Stay outside, crooked
villains', also clearly points to that conclusion). Incidentally, this reference does
not actually serve as a melody indication because there are no lyrics. Later in
this essay, I shall return to the intriguing question of why melody indications
are included in prose fiction at all.

   Prose texts from the 17th century with musical notation are extremely rare
(5). I found only two, the first of which is doubtful, as the music contained
therein is not actually part of the prose but is added as a separate attachment.
This is Mattheus Gansneb Tengnagel's translated novel *Het leven van Konstance*
from 1643, after Cervantes's *La Gitanilla*. The work contains a musical scene in
which there is supposed to be singing, but no text for the song is given. The same
collection, however, includes Tengnagel's play *Spaensche Heidin*, which is based on
the same novella and contains lyrics for that musical scene. The corresponding
musical notation is included at the end of the book, printed in two different
versions and with explicit mentioning of the name of the composer, Gerrit
Bolhamer. This is truly remarkable, as I have not encountered anything like it in
17th-century literature before, neither in prose works nor in play texts.

   The second example is in *De man in de maen* (1651) by Francis Godwin. The
original English novel, *The Man in the Moone* (1638), was already known in the
Netherlands shortly after its publication, as evidenced by a letter from Joan
Brosterhuysen to Constantijn Huygens in 1639.[15] Brosterhuysen was translating
the text at that time. The story is about Domingo Gonsales, 'the speedy mes-
senger', who goes to the moon in a kind of airplane *avant-la-lettre* pulled by geese.
His adventures on the moon are described, as are the people he meets there and
with whom he tries to talk. This is not a simple endeavour, as the people speak in
a strange way: they use an unusual language 'that is unrelated to any other language, because it does not consist of words and letters, but of tones: raw sounds
that cannot be expressed by letters'.[16] This quotation is a literal translation from
the Dutch edition (1651). The English original, on the other hand, has a slightly
different wording: 'First, because it hath no affinitie with any other that ever
I heard. Secondly, because it consisteth not so much of words and Letters as
of tunes and uncouth sounds, that no letters can expresse.'[17] Especially the part
on 'tunes' and 'tones' is striking. 'Toonen' in 17th-century Dutch means either
'tune' (melody) or (arranged) 'sound' (not raw sound), so at first the translation
does not seem dissimilar to the original. However, in the Dutch version the contrast between 'structured' and 'random' sound has been lost.

by exempel, fy hebben onder haer een ghewoonlijcke manier van groeten, betekenende nae de letter , *Gode zy alleen de Heerlickheydt*, het welck fy uyt-brengen (na dat ick 't verftae , want ick ben geen volkomen *Muficijn*) alleen met defe toonen , fonder een enckel woordt te fpreecken ;

- . Ja de Namen van Men*fchen* fullen fy op de felve wijfe uyt-drucken.
 Als 't haer lufte van my te fpreken in mijn by-wefen , fonder dat ick dat koft verftaen;dan was dit *Gonfales* te feggen:

Figure 9. Musical notation in Francis Godwin, *De Man in de Maen*, 1651. Amsterdam: Jacob Benjamin, p. 86. Allard Pierson, Universiteit van Amsterdam. OTM: OK 62-8672.

As far as the musical notation is concerned there are no differences. Two segments in the novel contain musical visualisations of how the phrase '*Gode zy alleen de Heerlickheydt*' ('To God only wise, be Glory') and the name 'Gonsales' sound in Lunar language.[18] The notation in the Dutch translation is exactly the same as the one in the English original.

For more insight into this matter – as I already said, examples from 17th-century Dutch sources are hard to find – it would be interesting to investigate the presence of musical notation in prose publications from later centuries. For example, the 18th-century collection of religious tales *Zedelyke uitspanningen* (1771) by Willem Hendrik Sels contains a 'Gezang' composed of ten verses, with a complete printed score.[19] The music is part of the first story, 'De geschiedenis van Atticus' ('The history of Atticus'). Two men are lying asleep in the wild and, upon waking, one of them begins to sing. Prior to the lyrics, which are included in their entirety, the narrator interrupts the story: 'I hope that the song will not displease the reader, and therefore I share it generously with him, simply as it is and as it fits Sincerus.'[20] In the preface to the collection, Sels, who himself lived on a remote estate in the province of Gelderland, had already revealed to the reader something about the origin of the music:

> There is no printing press in this region, only very far away. One of my friends who lives in Amsterdam (I also owe the song and epitaph to him) handled the printing himself. Thanks to him, these four stories shall see the light of day. They are adorned by two important masters, in etching and in the art of singing, and offer themselves here as too minor for envy and too serious for slander. They are made for my simple countrymen and neighbours, and only because we do not have a printing press here do they now appear before the eyes of exalted and clever minds, in one of the largest and most important commercial cities in our homeland.[21]

In terms of content, the scene is similar to that of earlier novels: a cheerful character (Sincerus) bursts into song while others – in this case, a melancholic opponent (Atticus) – marvel at that. Such concrete musical information from the 18th century might therefore, with retroactive effect, serve to clarify musical practices from 17th-century novels.

6

FUNCTIONS OF MUSIC IN 17TH-CENTURY DUTCH PROSE

In the preceding sections, I have broadly outlined the development of the presence of music in prose texts in the first half of the 17th century. I will now concentrate on the diverse ways in which the music appears in the novels. Roughly speaking, two categories can be distinguished, although more systematic research is needed in order to break down the various functions according to the types of prose in which music occurs. The first category involves music as a theme. This is the case when music plays a thematic role in a text (what Wolf refers to as 'thematization', 'telling' or 'explicit reference'). The second category involves music as a structural principle. This is the case when music has an impact on the form and structure of a text (Wolf speaks of 'imitation', 'showing' or 'implicit reference').[1]

The first category, music as a theme, includes all instances in which a prose text deals with music. This happens in a literal sense when the characters themselves speak of music. For example, 'He would rather listen to a drum or trumpet than a psalm, and he seemed to be born only for drinking and bloodshed.'[2] More specific examples include responses to certain music, for example, to a song that can be heard somewhere in the distance or that has just been heard without a visible source: 'O comrades, who is the damsel or goddess who plays the great vault of heaven and sings so pleasantly that the whole house reverberates?'[3] Even if the characters make no explicit reference to music, however, they sing, or dance and make music, either individually or collectively: 'They were singing in front of each other, holding each other by the hand, so that they could dance properly.'[4] Traditional musical instruments (e.g. trumpet, drum, harp, violin, lute, flute, gamba, zither, guitar) are played.[5] More unusual instruments are used as well: 'This hunting arrow was (simply put) an instrument that *Andronicus* often played to provide himself with music and cheerfulness, he called the thing (mockingly) *his cure for all kinds of diseases*.'[6] In the farcical Cervantes translation *Monipodios Hol* (1658), everyday objects are used as musical instruments:

Klim-op took off his shoes, and began to play energetically; *Win-al* took a new palm broom, which he found by chance, and began to make a hoarse sound with it, which still went well with the shoe music. *Monipodio* smashed a saucer and stuck two of the shards like castanets between his fingers, and began to play them masterfully, under the bass and tenor of the shoe and broom.[7]

The fragment originates from the only extensive musical scene in this text. Later in the work, a character speaks extensively about the use of music in pastoral and romance novels. What makes this speech especially interesting is that the first-person narrator remembers having heard such books read aloud:

That my Master's mistress, when I was in the house with her, used to read books that were about nothing but shepherds and shepherdesses, and that she said they were singing and playing bagpipes, violins, clanging toys, reed flutes, and other strange instruments all their lives. I listened to her words sometimes. I heard that the shepherd *Amfrisius* sang so beautifully. And that he raised his incomparable Belizarde to the stars, yes, that there was not a tree on the mountains of all Arcadia under which he had not sung, from the moment the sun rose from the arms of *Aurora* until it was again returned to *Thetis'* arms, and that even the night, covering the earth with its brown wings, did not prevent him from always expressing himself in beautifully sung laments. Yes, I remember hearing her read several of those books.[8]

The ever-singing shepherds are reminiscent of Cervantes's *Don Quixote*, in which, at some point, the endless pastoral singing is discussed by the characters. The priest and barber, who have been left in a mountain gorge by Sancho Panza, suddenly hear someone singing in the peace and quiet: a pleasant sound 'which they were very much surprised by, because they assumed that this was not exactly a place where you would expect such singing. After all, it is said that in forests and fields you sometimes find shepherdesses who can sing particularly beautifully, although this is the knowledge and experience of poets rather than the truth.'[9] In other words, as the novels say, within the story, fiction suddenly reveals itself to be reality.

Many novels contain one or more examples of such musical scenes. A story could also be all about music, for instance through the introduction of a musical protagonist. In Cervantes's *Den Ialoerssen Carrizale* (the Dutch version of *El celoso extremeño* from 1643), a musical character appears and dominates the entire act – in this case, a 'Sangh-meester' (singing teacher). I have been unable to find any other original Dutch prose works with such

Figure 10. Jan Lievens, *Two Women with a Book in a Landscape*, undated (17th century). Etching. Rijksmuseum Amsterdam RP-P-OB-12.603.

an all-dominating musical main character. Towards the end of the century, however, there are several German examples of texts devoted to music, by Johann Beer, Wolfgang Caspar Printz and Johann Kuhnau – three writers who were also performing musicians. Kuhnau, for example, wrote a satirical novel entitled *Musicalischer Quacksalber* (1700), which is about a German musician who is infatuated with Italian music.[10] I have not encountered any dual literary–musical talents like this amongst Dutch authors. In fiction, however, we do meet them as characters who are either writers or singers (or both at the same time). As writers these characters are always men who command

the admiration of their audience with their songs and poems. This is not surprising, in the context of a period that was characterised by a vibrant oral
tradition in which the ability to write was not taken for granted, especially
as far as poetry is concerned.[11] With regard to singing, in fictional texts men
and women tend to be especially admired for their talent for singing – the
possession of a beautiful voice testified to a noble character. This is in fact an
age-old *topos*: perfect art can be produced only by people whose conduct is
exemplary.[12]

The ancient power of music is an important novelistic theme. The wind
stops blowing when there is singing in the air. The singing itself is 'like the
sound of swans, or similar birds, and as the murmur of western winds and
streams of water'.[13] There is 'the power of sorcery' regarding the sound of a
horn from which a whole crowd of people flees in panic:

> They scattered en masse, with one trampling the other. Some lost their
> lives in the crowd, while others jumped from the racks and the windows
> and fell to death. Many broke their necks and arms. Some lay dead on
> the ground, others were paralysed. The sighing and screaming, accom-
> panied by a sound of crushing and breaking, rose to the heavens. The
> fearsome rabble turned away quickly from the side where the sound of
> the horn came from.[14]

The excerpt comes from the Dutch translation of Ariosto's *Orlando Furioso*
(1510), in which the musical instrument thus acts as a kind of weapon of
war with explosive power. Bagpipers can also be thought of in this context
because in reality they often led the charge in battle. Music is violent in a
physical sense, but it is striking to note how intense the reactions of characters
are when they hear music. Usually, it is rather the other way around. Instead
of being driven away, the listeners are lured by the sound. There are many
examples of love or enchantment at the first sound of music, as well as of
characters who hear someone sing in the distance and are completely surprised or deeply touched.[15] In Van Hoogstraten's *Schone Rooseliin* (1650), the
two friends Panthus and Damor unexpectedly witness a duet between a night-
ingale and an invisible singer:

> He comforted his friend as best he could, promising that he would do
> his best, and while he was busy telling of his own freedom and accusing
> Rooseliin while also playing the victim somewhat, they heard (while the
> nightingale made the trees in the forest sound like organ pipes) someone
> who, while singing, remained down by the creek.[16]

The men are delighted: they descend to the stream, approach the singer and ask him about the cause of his joy. He replies that singing does not always come from joy, 'as the glorious Poet *Hooft* says through his *Dorilea*' – upon which he recites the passage from the play *Granida* (1615) by the famous Amsterdam poet and playwright Pieter Cornelisz Hooft:

> When the courtiers
> Sing a cheerful song,
> Then it is not of joy,
> But to make the grief that
> torments the heart,
> Somewhat less burdensome.[17]

The reactions of listeners to music are often intense, especially where singing is involved.[18] In Baltes Boekholt's *De wonderlijke vryagien* (1668), a woman, Narsisa, meets a group of gypsies. While they are in conversation, she hears from behind a hill 'the sound of a zither so sweet in the ears that Narsisa's heart was taken by it, and she was beside herself with delight when she heard the sound of a voice and the instrument blend into each other'. The song that thus puts a spell on her is sung by a male voice, to the melody of 'La belle Iris'.[19] Another vivid example can be found in De Rosset's *Waerachtige treurige geschiedenissen onzes tijdts* (1632): the beautiful Fleurie sings a love song with her 'divine voice' while she accompanies herself on the lute. A young nobleman who happens to be walking along the river hears her singing and is so enchanted by 'this beautiful sun, who played on the instrument and sang so melodiously', that he faints upon seeing her. Surprised, the damsels arrive, startled by the worried sound of his sighs and by his dramatic collapse.[20] Three examples of a song being overheard: in early modern prose fiction it was a popular technique to set a story going. It reflects earlier times and can already be found in Giovanni Boccaccio's *Il Ninfale d'Ameto* (1341).[21]

Such vehement physical reactions to music are found more often in the earlier prose texts. For example, in Nicolaas Heinsius's *Don Clarazel de Gontarnos* (1697), the Marquis is sitting on the toilet when he suddenly hears music, so pleasant that it immediately affects the condition of his intestines, and he wants to get to the bottom of his discomfort as soon as possible:

> The flux of our *Marquis* suddenly turned costive when, in the heart of his defecation, such pleasing *music* found its way to his ears. After having thrown a couple of eggs in the bowl and keeping the process of pressing as quick as possible, he went into the direction of the room where he heard the sound coming from.[22]

Unfortunately, he is denied access to the music room, and he becomes furious. Why are such reactions to music so excessive? Characters who listen are carried away by the singing of other characters. Readers, in turn, are able to wallow in the passionate response of these fictional listeners. These listeners are usually presented as appealing characters who are admired for their artistic sensitivity.[23] They were also highly regarded because of their capacity for 'transport, ecstasy, and enthusiasm'.[24] People like to read about such emotions. The ability to lose oneself in another world is something that people have desired throughout the ages.

Up to this point, we have covered the ways in which music is thematically intertwined with prose. In a later section, I will come back to the question as to how such fictional descriptions of musical behaviour and habits relate to the reality of the times. First, however, I would like to focus on the second category: the structuring functions of music, by which I mean the ways in which music can influence the form of a text. Imitation of musical forms in literature did not exist in the 17th century. At that time, no attempt was made to write prose in the form of a sonata or a fugue, or, for example, to mimic the associative character of music in language. In other words, there was no question of formal and structural analogies to music, as would be the case from the beginning of the 20th century.[25] What was a musically significant aspect of the prose during the earlier period, however, was the frequent insertion of lyrics. This practice can also be observed in today's novels, but not to the extent to which or in the same way as it was used in early modern prose texts.[26] In the 17th century, authors either used existing songs or wrote new texts set to existing melodies. The latter, the so-called 'contrafacts', were most common in Dutch prose fiction works.

From an international perspective the insertion of contrafacts in prose fiction was not unusual – although incorporation of complete songs clearly prevailed in other European countries. The aforementioned trend of providing associated melody indications, however, was exceptional. To the best of my knowledge, it was not done anywhere else, and seems to be a phenomenon restricted to the 17th-century Dutch situation (this is in fact an aspect which applies to the theatre as well: songs in Dutch stage plays are mainly contrafacts, whereas playwrights elsewhere in Europe inserted complete songs, 'snatches of ballads' or newly composed songs).[27]

First proof or evidence for this statement can be found in the prose works themselves, that is, by comparing some novellas and novels translated into Dutch to translations of the same texts into other languages. Consider, for instance, the song from Cervantes's *El celoso extremeño*, as discussed above. The Dutch translation *Den Ialoersen Carrizale* (1643) contains a melody indication that does not appear in the French (1615) or English (1709) translations, or

Figure 11. Image of a musical scene in Vital d'Audiguier, *Lysander en Caliste*, 1663. Amsterdam: Baltes Boeckholt, between pp. 104–05. Engraving. Koninklijke Bibliotheek, National Library of the Netherlands. 2202 G 21.

in the Spanish original (1613). This later 18th-century English version also reveals a further interesting fact, namely that it used to be customary to insert new songs for new translations of the same prose texts that were made over time. These must have been songs that were currently popular, and this practice must have been applied in the literature of the Netherlands as well.[28] The way lies open here for further research.

A second example is the popular *Histoire trage-comique de nostre temps, sous les noms de Lysandre et de Caliste* by Vital d'Audiguier (1616). This French novel was frequently reprinted and translated in the 17th century. In the Netherlands alone, it had appeared under the title *De treurige doch bly-eyndigende historie van onsen tijdt, onder de naem van Lysander en Caliste* in at least six editions (1632, 1636, 1658, 1666, 1669, 1703), in addition to three bilingual editions (1650, 1663, 1670). In 1663, a stage adaptation by Johan Blasius was published, and D'Audiguier's text was translated not only into Dutch but also into English (1621, 1627, 1635, 1652), German (1644, 1650, 1670) and Italian (1663, 1671). The use of music in this novel can therefore be studied from both a genre-transcending and a European perspective.[29] In addition to a number of fictional letters, the novel contains five songs.[30] Here the original text will be compared to the German, English and Dutch translations from 1644, 1652 and 1663, respectively. The German translation from 1644 is by Philipp von Zesen, who was a novelist himself. In 1645, he published the first original German novel *Adriatische Rosemund*. His *Liebes-Beschreibung Lysanders und Kalisten* was published a year earlier by the Elzevier publishing house in Amsterdam. The entire text is printed in Gothic type, and there are no typographical distinctions between the running prose text and the inserted lyrics. The translation contains four songs. There is no musical notation, nor are there any tune indications. In two cases, the stanzas are numbered.[31] The English translation *Lisander and Calista* from 1652 appeared anonymously in an abridged version. The text contains three songs, also without music notation or tune indications.[32] The Dutch translation of 1663 is by Jacob Heerman, who, as a French translator, had been known since the 1630s for his translations of parts from D'Urfé's *L'Astrée*. Like the French text, his *Lysander en Caliste* contains five songs. Music notation is lacking here as well. Unlike the French original, however, melody indications are given for four of the songs.[33] The play *Lysander en Kaliste* by Johan Blasius, which addresses the same material and was added to the 1663 edition, also contains several songs with tune indications.[34]

The next question is why tune indications were mentioned at all. Given that these melodies were used to create new Dutch lyrics, they might have been intended to help the translators. If this were the case, however, what would be the reason for their not being removed from the final printed text? Moreover, why would translators have gone to so much trouble? They surely would have been able to translate the original lyrics into Dutch without thinking about the music, just as their predecessors had done in the first decades of the century.

Perhaps we should look at this issue from a slightly broader perspective. It is particularly interesting to see how the development of music in Dutch prose fiction ties in with the song culture in the Netherlands at the time.[35] During the period there was a great deal of singing: everyone sang – everywhere and always – be they rich, poor, young or old. Popular songs resounded on the streets and in people's homes. They were sung and played, on carillons, in

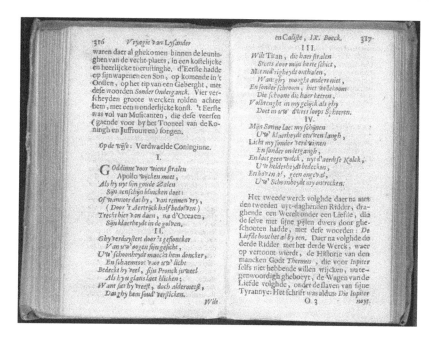

Figure 12. Song with tune indication in Vital d'Audiguier, *Lysander en Caliste*, 1663. Amsterdam: Baltes Boeckholt, pp. 316–17. Koninklijke Bibliotheek, National Library of the Netherlands. 2202 G 21.

music inns, at parties, weddings, in churches and theatres. They also found their way into other literary genres, including stage plays and epic poems. This all-pervading singing was common throughout Europe, people knew hundreds of melodies by heart and audiences needed only a brief hint to know what music was about to be played and sung. Marsh rightly points out that to us this phenomenon may seem rather incredible: 'It may be difficult for us to accept that many members of the target audience were sufficiently musical to recall dozens of tunes, learn new ones and fit fresh texts to them all, but it is equally difficult to explain why the system prevailed for so long if this were not the case.'[36] Songs were broadly disseminated on printed broadsides, usually consisting of a song text, a woodcut and a tune indication. Musical notation was rarely included.[37] Tune indications made it possible for many to sing a text – the early modern public was accustomed to this type of participation. The songs were also collected in songbooks, a genre which became widespread, especially in the Netherlands: hundreds of song compilations were published and sold in all manner of sizes and prices, a rich harvest now preserved in libraries and a fascinating collection that is unique in Europe for

Figure 13. Jan de Bisschop, *Portrait of Jacobus van Ewijk Reading a Book,* undated (17th century). Brush in brown over a sketch with black chalk, some pencil. Rijksmuseum Amsterdam RP-T-1905-50.

both its quality and quantity. Nowhere else were songbooks so popular and widely distributed as in the Netherlands.[38] One of the advantages of this special legacy in which occasionally musical notation can also be found is that quite a lot of tunes have been preserved that would otherwise have been lost.[39] The study of music in Dutch prose fiction can obviously benefit from this.

Let us now return to the song in literature and, more specifically, to songs with tune indications that occur in prose fiction. The preceding discussion might seem to suggest that references to melodies might have been more of a helping hand for the reading audience than a tool for translators. It might also suggest that the melody indications reveal something about the actual use of prose texts during the period. Any more definitive statements in this regard would require additional information about the reading culture in the Golden Age.

7

READING NOVELS IN THE 17TH CENTURY

We do know a few things about the manner in which prose texts were read in the 17th century. Especially in recent years, considerable research has focused on reader response, in contrast to earlier scholarship that concentrated more on 'what' was read rather than 'how' it was read.[1] The 'how' of reading is of particular importance with regard to the 17th century, as indicated by Isabelle Moreau in *Seventeenth-Century Fiction* (2016): 'How prose fiction was read is as important to determine as what was read in the first place. The reader's expectations are central to seventeenth-century poetics, and become even more so when considered across generic, linguistic, and geo-political boundaries.'[2]

One thing is clear, however, about reading behaviour in the 17th century: reading at that time was in many ways different from reading today.[3] Individual reading was done in two ways: either silently (possibly while moving the lips and perhaps muttering) or aloud.[4] An example of reading aloud can be found in the diary of David Beck, a schoolmaster from The Hague, who wrote in 1624 that a friend had unexpectedly visited him in the evening: 'while he heard me read in the *Self-strijt* for a while'.[5]

Collective reading consisted of either reading to others or being read to. Examples of reading to others can also be found in the diary of David Beck, who wrote about reading his own poems to his family and friends, and about reading aloud from books. To a close friend he recited a 'part of the book *Mespris de la Cour* and from the *Parfaite amye* by A. Herroet' (two 16th-century texts dedicated to the position of women).[6]

In such cases one person reads aloud, while one or more others listen.[7] In that sense, reading is different from singing, which can be done by several people at once. The effect on the listener may be the same, however. Stories about reading aloud to people who are so impressed that they begin to tremble, cry, faint or lose their minds are well known. A remarkable anecdote that has come down to us from 17th-century reality describes how a woman started laughing so uncontrollably while listening to a story that her contractions began, and within three hours she gave birth to her child.[8] The following passage from *Don Quixote*, in which the innkeeper talks about how workers come together to listen to the reading of a romance of chivalry, provides an interesting literary example:

> I only have two or three of these books and they enrich my life. And not just mine, but also the lives of many others. When it is harvest time, many workers gather here on religious holidays, and there is always one around who can read. He then takes one of these books, and we sometimes sit around him with thirty people and listen with such focus that we cannot think of anything else anymore. For myself, I can say that I could listen day and night, to the terrible battles the knights have fought and to the wonderful adventures they experience. The innkeeper's wife agreed to that. I have no more peace in my house than when my husband is listening, he does not make a peep, while he normally only grumbles and mumbles. And what do you think of it, child? said the priest to the daughter of the innkeeper. What shall I say, sir, answered the young girl. Although I don't understand everything, I still enjoy it a lot. Not those terrible battles my father mentioned, but the despair of the knights when they miss their loved ones. They sometimes make me cry with pity.[9]

Reading aloud was a common practice for centuries. Wealthy Romans had already been read to by their literate slaves.[10] Reading aloud at a party could count as a gift to the host.[11] In monasteries, the rule of Benedict required (as it still does) one of the monks to read aloud during dinner: 'At the table there is complete silence, so that no one's murmur or voice can be heard, only that of the reader.'[12] Dutch fathers also read to their offspring from the Bible at the table.[13] In the 17th century family reading was even regarded as an acceptable alternative to church visits.[14] Furthermore, it is known that the 18th-century French writer and philosopher Denis Diderot read to his wife to cure her of her low spirits:

> I have become her Reader. I administer three pinches of *Gil Blas* every day: one in the morning, one after dinner, and one in the evening. When we have seen the end of *Gil Blas*, we shall go on to *The Devil on Two Sticks* and *The Bachelor of Salamanca* and other cheering works of the same class. A few years and a few hundred such readings will complete the cure. If I were sure of success, I should not complain at the labour. What amuses me is that she treats everyone who visits her to a repeat of what I have just read to her, so the conversation doubles

the effect of the remedy. I have always spoken of novels as frivolous productions, but I have finally discovered that they are good for the vapours.[15]

Figure 14. Daniel Nikolaus Chodowiecki, *Father Reading to His Children by Candlelight,* 1800 (detail). Etching. Rijksprentenkabinet Amsterdam RP-P-OB-115.699.

Members of the military read to each other in the evening after work. Women did this during work, while spinning, sewing or weaving. It was crucial for women to do so because their handicrafts and household duties left them with much less time than men to read in solitude (obviously this varied according to their social class and education). In advice books, such as James Fordice's *Vriend der jonge juffrouwen* (*Friend of the Young Ladies*) (1767), reading aloud was strongly recommended as an appropriate thing to do during work.[16] Merchant ships of the 17th century usually had a reader on board, as was the case for the ship on which skipper Willem IJsbrandtsz Bontekoe sailed between 1618 and 1625. In his *Journael ofte gedenckwaerdige beschrijvinghe van de Oost-Indische reijse* he writes: 'We devoutly prayed in the morning and evening to God and sang a psalm before and after prayer, for we had some psalmbooks with us. Usually I was the reader, but later, when the reader came back to our vessel from the barge, he did it himself.'[17] In Cuban cigar factories during the second half of the 19th century, a special reader (*el lector*) was appointed to help ease the monotonous rolling work.[18] Also, in the 20th century, during protracted operations in hospitals, someone would read from a book. And of course, even now, children are still being read to by their parents or nannies. 'We first experience reading before we can read ourselves.'[19]

In the 17th century, reading aloud was at once a much-loved pastime and a necessity. Few people could read and, if they could, there was often too little money to buy books. Literacy in Europe was low at that time, though it was relatively high in the Netherlands.[20] Still, it is a difficult thing to measure. Circulation figures for books do not provide much useful information, if only because, in practice, the use of a book was rarely limited to one person: there were always several people who read or heard it.[21] Sometimes, an illiterate person would buy a book and then have someone else read it aloud.[22] We must therefore proceed cautiously when interpreting the accessibility of printed matter. Although it had become abundantly available for sale by that time, with plenty of books, pamphlets and song sheets, nonetheless this vast amount of material circulated within a culture that still was largely 'orally' organised. Street singers, market merchants, clergymen, peddlers and lectors would speak their words aloud, both indoors and outdoors, and this kind of oral practice remained ubiquitous until well into the 18th century.[23] In the latter century reading aloud as a domestic pursuit became increasingly popular, and many people were using instruction manuals in their efforts to improve their declamation.[24] Nowadays we have modern counterparts like podcasts and audiobooks (the history of which, by the way, has recently become a subject of study as well).[25] These new means can provide some sense of earlier reading practices, but in the end they do not do much to bring back the past. Life in the 17th century remains to a great extent a mystery, like another realm, only partly accessible to us.

'Oral behaviour' is a term that applies equally to the literate and to the illiterate. People liked reading to each other, even within environments in which many people were able to read for themselves.[26] This was the case especially for writers, for whom it would long remain a habit to read new work to friends prior to publication, in order to gauge their reaction. For example, we know that, in 1849, over the course of four days Gustave Flaubert read the complete manuscript of his novel *La Tentation de St. Antoine* to his friends Maxime du Camp and Louis Bouilhet (whose devastating conclusion was, 'You have to throw the whole thing into the fire and never think about it again').[27] For others, reading aloud was a popular pastime which

Figure 15. Moses ter Borch, *Soldier Reading to his Colleague*, ca. 1662. Drawing. Rijksmuseum Amsterdam RP-T-1887-A-1333(R).

was also an important part of social life.[28] In addition to the well-known example of the French literary salons, there were several other groups in which collective reading was practised. The Netherlands had its famous chambers of rhetoric in the cities, as well as less organised clubs such as the literary friends who visited the Amsterdam poet Pieter Cornelisz Hooft at the Muiderslot, his summer home in Muiden. These gatherings consisted of well-tried forms of artistic and intellectual sociability. Also, reading aloud was a favourite activity within the smaller context of family, loved ones and friends. People read to each other from books and newspapers. They even had personal manuscripts especially for this purpose, containing a potpourri of texts collected from books or self-written poems and songs.[29] David Beck mentions in his diary that he had narrated the complete contents of two novels to his friends – this time not by reading, but by summarising them from memory.[30] This is interesting information, given that, for the early modern period, storytelling is usually associated with village culture and reading aloud with urban culture.[31] However, it is difficult to draw sharp dividing lines between what is sometimes called 'the private reading habits of the elites' and 'the collective reading habits of the common people': 'Learned reading could still be reading in common or reading aloud.'[32] Of course Beck might have been an exception in this regard, given the fact that he was a schoolmaster.

The focus on reading aloud meant that readers were expected to have an expressive manner of declamation, in order to project emotion and evoke audience response. Moreover, the practice also had a beneficial side effect for the reader, as reading aloud was considered good for one's health. It stimulated physical activity in the head, chest and arms.[33] According to various sources, readers had to be able to portray different characters through voice and gesture.[34] Some early texts include explicit reading instructions to this end. In *La Celestina* (1500), an example of Italian prose fiction, there is a poem at the end of the book which advises the reader to pronounce all asides with a soft voice ('one has to know to talk between one's teeth') and to vary in pitch while reading ('sometimes with gaiety, hope and passion, sometimes angry, in despair'). These directions were intended to captivate the audience in *mil artes y modos* ('a thousand ways and manners').[35] In this way, reading aloud became a 'performance', comparable to play-acting and, particularly, to singing and music making, as noted by Guglielmo Cavallo and Roger Chartier in their *History of Reading in the West*: 'Not surprisingly, the verb for poetic reading is often *cantare*. Reading a literary text could be compared to performing from a musical score.'[36] In his article about music in Laurence Sterne's *Tristram Shandy*, Daniel Hocutt wrote about 'the musical nature of performed text'.[37] Daniel R. Woolf also emphasised 'this vocal conception of the intercourse between an absent author, living or dead, and his or her reader' in his *Reading History in Early Modern England*.[38] This is consistent with what has been concluded by literary historians of medieval texts, that 'performative reading' is crucial to the understanding of early prose works. And also in the early modern field the resistance to a performance-based analysis of literature is shifting, as the aforementioned studies by Richards and Larson convincingly attest.[39] Moreover, Richards prefers the term 'vocality' instead of 'orality', because too often 'oral' and 'orality' relate to 'illiterate' and 'illiteracy', and also because 'vocal' includes the internal voice as well as the physical voice: 'I am proposing that the oral/aural context of reading in this period produced voice- or performance-aware silent readers as well as readers who literally animated the page with their breath.'[40] In *Music and Society in Early Modern England* (2010) Christopher Marsh pointed to this as well: 'Even silent reading was probably imagined as sound, for early modern people felt more acutely than we do that "writing is no more than the image or character of speech".'[41] According to Richards attention to vocality 'fundamentally changes the way we interpret the texts and books of the past, silently or aloud'.[42] Larson also calls for a 'more elastic analysis of early modern texts': although we cannot attend the original presentations, this 'does not mean that the unfixed and evanescent nature of performance refuses analysis entirely'.[43]

Figure 16. Hendrik Bary, *Three Men at a Table Discussing a Book*, 1662. In Jacobus Sceperus, *Chrysopolipoimeen, dat is Goutsche herder*, Amsterdam (detail title page). Engraving. Rijksmuseum Amsterdam. RP-P-1884-A-7944.

Given what has been mentioned previously with regard to reading aloud, it might seem that the level was high at the time. Thus far, however, I have not been able to find any evidence, at least not for the 17th-century Dutch situation. For the 18th century evidence does exist, however. A passage in the *Economische liedjes* (1781) by Betje Wolff and Aagje Deken addresses the issue in detail, but their final assessment is not exactly reassuring. Indeed, they describe the level of reading at the time as downright awful. According to them, it would be better to encourage people to sing:

Most people read so badly, it's tragic to hear. People, especially poets, who write beautifully and well themselves, read their verses to us in such a poor way that a man would not wish it on his worst enemy. The reading can make texts incredibly attractive or completely destroy them. We give them to the good congregation, which usually reads just as badly as the schoolmaster himself, who taught it the little bit he knew but in a very imperfect way. Not everyone has a good voice, yet one still finds twenty good singers to one good reader.[44]

In the meantime, the 'vocal' element of literature had consequences not only for readers but also for writers. Texts had to be suitable for oral presentation (or vocal imagination), meaning that for a long time the 'old' oral tradition continued to influence the manner in which new texts were written. In terms of content, an involuntarily emphasis on orality already existed, given that lyrics from the 16th and 17th centuries contain a 'much greater frequency of metaphors of sound rather than sight'.[45] The oral function was also revealed in the style and composition of works: 'Prose style had a very "oral" quality, a high degree of colloquialism and formularity.'[46] Moreover, prose texts contained a wide array of indications for oral presentation, ranging from 'the insertion of textual cues that guide the reader towards oral or corporal performance' to 'rhetorical devices (pauses, exclamations etc.)'.[47] 'All of these verbal strategies reveal that [he] was quite rooted in oral techniques similar to those employed in public storytelling,' as Gasta specifically writes about Cervantes's *Don Quixote*.[48] Richards also recognises the importance of vocal performance marks in English Renaissance texts: she argues that 'the printed page need to be looked at with fresh eyes. It is full of cues for reading aloud'.[49] Abigail Williams emphasises that such indications for shared reading can be found in both the materiality and content of books: 'Print sizes, book formats, and genres of writing were shaped by their suitability for performance. Large text, small books, short extracts, episodic structure, epigrammatic snippets: all made text more portable or more adaptable for use in company.'[50]

Furthermore, it is especially striking that many texts from this period address the oral presentation itself as a theme.[51] Sometimes, it is merely discussed by the characters, but more often a fictional situation is created in which characters turn to an audience while reading their poems and stories aloud. So, even in printed fiction there was apparently a need for a narrator who could address a real or imaginary public.[52] This point is often made at the very beginning of a book, as is traditionally the case in medieval texts. The famous opening lines of *Karel ende Elegast* are a case in point:

> Listen, I will tell you
> A beautiful and true story
> It was one night
> That Karel went to sleep...
> Hear this miracle and truth
> Of what happened to the king
> Many still remember it.[53]

In addition to this well-tried method, 17th-century prose writers and publishers developed other ways of achieving the effect of orality. For example, images

Figure 17. Jan Luyken, *Man Reading to Three Pilgrims in Front of a Straw Hut*, 1687 (detail). Etching. Rijksmuseum Amsterdam RP-P-1896-A-19368-652.

on title pages often depict an actor or narrator on a stage with curtains on both sides.[54] Writers also liked to present their stories as fictional autobiographies, in which an actor or adventurer – real or imagined – told the audience stories. Particularly intriguing are the prose texts in which a fictional manuscript is revealed within the story, and in which a large part of the text then consists of reading and singing from it. Finally, the frame story was quite popular. It consists of a fixed narrative form in which a group of characters at a given location entertained each other for hours, days and, sometimes, even weeks with stories, poetry and music. Within the fictional setting of the 'frame', various texts could be recited and sung to the heart's content. All of these forms were literary tricks: they allowed for a lively reading, while also producing a kind of 'logical hybridity'.

Examples of such frame narratives include the medieval Middle Eastern *Arabian Nights*, with Scheherazade saving her own life by telling stories for 'one thousand and one nights' to King Shahryar, and Boccaccio's *Decamerone* (1353), in which seven women and three men entertain each other with stories and songs for 10 days during the plague epidemic in Florence in order to dispel fear and boredom.[55] *Cent Nouvelles Nouvelles* (1465) consists of 100 stories told by different characters at the court of Philips the Good. In *Les évangiles des quenouilles* (1480) a group of women read to each other for six days; in between they wind the yarn and comment on the things that have been read. Straparola's *Le piacevoli notti* (1550) is about a high-class group of young men and women who entertain each other for thirteen nights with dance, song, stories and riddles during the 1536 carnival. The *Heptaméron* (1558), Giambattista Basile's *Pentamerone* (1634) and Cervantes's *Don Quixote* (1605) provide further examples, and as Chad Gasta notes, 'most texts within the frame of *Don Quixote* are read aloud, not silently', thereby drawing our attention to 'the performative nature of the entire novel'.[56] In addition, Chartier concludes that Cervantes goes beyond the frame: '[He] plays in a variety of ways with the motif of reading aloud and its corollary, an audience listening to the text being read.'[57] I have already quoted the innkeeper who tells us that, in harvest time, a novel was read to some thirty workers. Elsewhere in the book, the manuscript of a novel is revealed, and the reading of this imagined novel then proceeds in the next three chapters.[58] Inside the main frame, new frames are created that allow much more reading aloud and singing.

8

FICTION AND REALITY

It is clear that reading prose texts aloud was not just a popular pastime in the Netherlands during the 17th century – it functioned also as a kind of *topos* in prose fiction itself. Characters in the novels often 'vocalised' (i.e. read aloud and sang) and the frame story was particularly suited to this. Consequently, the frame story was much favoured in this context, and it always had the same structure, with a group of people put 'on stage' to tell each other stories and to read and sing together. Usually this takes place at a specified location, such as the various Dutch towns in the *Nederduytsche Helicon* (1610), or at the unnamed polder near Amsterdam, in Cornelis Danckertsz's *Nutte Tijdtquistingh der Amstelsche Jonckheyt* (1640).[1] In this novel some good-hearted friends spend their time 'playing sweet games, asking each other profound questions, sharing riddles, playing, singing' and telling each other stories that they had heard or read somewhere.[2] Before that, however, they start their hours-long gathering by reading aloud a new book, which one of them had just translated from the French: 'De Turksche Historie van de desperate Orcane en Erremonde' ('The Turkish history of the desperate Orcane and Erremonde').[3] The frame could therefore describe a location, and also engage us in a journey. In the latter case, the characters would read and sing while they are on the road, as happens in Jacob van Heemskerck's *Batavische Arcadia* (1637) and also in Hendrick Soeteboom's *Zaanlants Arkadia* (1658).[4] A famous foreign example in this category is Chaucer's *The Canterbury Tales* (ca. 1400), a wonderful collection of tales that is presented as a story-telling contest by a group of pilgrims as they travel together from London to Canterbury.

In farce books and song collections of the period, this kind of collective entertainment is often depicted in the title illustrations, which show groups of people holding the books in question, possibly sharing jokes or singing together. In prose, the frame structure is also used for a similar purpose, although an illustration depicting a collective reading is rarely found in prose texts. Still, a frame narrative is not required for an oral performance within a novel. In scenes which are not contained by any specific frame, characters nonetheless entertain each other with stories, poems and songs. The examples presented here could be supplemented by dozens of others. Some prose texts contain

Figure 18. Anonymous, *Woman Reading a Book Under a Tree*, 1650–1700. Etching. Rijksmuseum Amsterdam RP-P-1879-A-3651.

so many inserted passages that, in terms of 'vocal performance', their form differs little from that of a proper frame narrative.

A relevant question at this point concerns the way prose fiction was read at the time. We know that the characters within the stories were constantly reading aloud – reciting, telling tales and singing. Did the actual readers of those books do the same? As was made clear before, reading in groups was quite common, and these groups were of many kinds: women, men, individually or together, at home, on the road, in church, at school, in the family, during work or for entertainment and relaxation. In this respect, the fictional situations depict reality, as is also pointed out by Chartier: 'Certain works of fiction depict reading aloud, as performed by a reader vocalising a text for an assembly of listeners grouped about him, to be a common method of circulating the work.'[5] Reality and fiction overlap in other ways as well. For example, in the Netherlands, people like David Beck, who – like their male counterparts in the novels – produced poems and songs at the request of friends.[6] Although

Figure 19. Esaias van de Velde (possibly), *Young Couple Reading a Book*, 1625–30. Brush in grey and brown, black chalk. Rijksmuseum Amsterdam RP-T-1893-A-2766(V).

they might not have been admired so glowingly as their fictional fellow poets, they certainly gained in respect and standing.

Another striking similarity between fiction and reality is the smooth transition (or, perhaps, blurred separation) between reading and singing. This phenomenon appears repeatedly and in a variety of ways in 17th-century prose texts. In Jean Desmarets's *D'onvergelijkelijke Ariane* (1646), the recitation of a poem seamlessly changes over to the singing of a song. Poem and song are interconnected by an intermediate text that acts as a kind of stage direction:

> Lepante, who had come to the landing with Cyllenia and the others, heard Melinte recite the verses he had just created. At the same time, he quickly finished and immediately recited his new verses, and when he found a lute, he added his voice to the sound of this instrument, and sang the lines as follows.[7]

One more question concerns whether poetic asides – such as 'my throat is hoarse from such a deep voice' in Samuel van Hoogstraten's novel *Haegaenveld* (1669) – were meant to be exclusively metaphorical (specifically pertaining to the narrator) or whether they were also intended as literal (referring specifically to the reader).[8]

Finally, in the novels it is not always clear which strophic and/or italicised passages were meant to be sung and which were not. Typically spoken poetic forms (e.g. the sonnet) could apparently serve as songs in some sources.[9] As noted by Cathy Elias in an article on the 16th-century Italian frame narrative *Le piacevoli notti*, '*dire* is sometimes equivalent to *cantare*'.[10] Larson also points to this phenomenon when she discusses the use of the verb 'deliver' in Lady Mary Wroth's prose romance *The Countess of Montgomery's Urania* (1621) – a word that could mean either 'to recite' or 'to utter notes in singing'.[11] Speaking can mean singing, and singing is sometimes speaking. In some 17th-century Dutch songbooks, this dual function of lyrics was even explicitly required. For example, a collection by Cornelis de Leeuw was entitled *Christelyke plicht-rymen om te singen of te leesen* (*Christian Devotion Verses to Sing or Read*) (1649). In addition, in the foreword to his *Stichtelycke rymen. Om te lezen of te zingen* (1624), Dirk Rafaelsz Camphuysen advocates that 'all rhymes' should be written 'in order to be both read and sung: every verse or poem must be (according to old usage and also in the nature of things) both readable and singable, or both singable and readable'.[12]

9

SINGING WHILE READING

Let us now return to prose fiction. We know that novels were read aloud and that lectors were expected to render a convincing and compelling reading, with variations in pitch and the use of different voices. The next question then would be: were they also expected to perform the songs from the novels?[1] That might be the case. On the one hand, the prose fiction excerpts describe an ideal situation, a dreamed-of world in which people could immerse themselves imaginatively, to which they were able to turn for some relief from their everyday lives, and from which they could find inspiration.[2] On the other hand, the texts also reflect social interactions at that time. Coming together for entertainment with books and music was not only a popular theme in literature but also an everyday activity in which speaking and singing often merged seamlessly with each other. In the course of an evening, people would read aloud from a novel, recite a few poems and, finally, sing a few songs or psalms.

The next step is to consider whether singing would occur *during* the reading. We do not yet know the answer to this question. However, there is evidence from an earlier period in which there was such a tradition: narrative texts from the Middle Ages are known to have been spoken and sung. However, Karl Reichl has pointed out, in his contribution to Vitz and Regalado's survey *Performing Medieval Narrative* (2005), that specific knowledge about the execution is still largely lacking for this repertoire.[3] Maureen Barry McCann Boulton also addressed the issue in *The Song in the Story: Lyric Insertions in French Narrative Fiction, 1200–1400* (1993): 'Were the songs actually meant to be sung in these new contexts? An affirmative answer is indicated by much of the textual and manuscript evidence.'[4] She points, inter alia, to the presence of musical notation in a number of manuscripts, and observes that 'even without notation [...] lyric insertions differ from the surrounding narrative in that they imply performance, even in the absence of performers'.[5] She is unable, however, to provide a definitive answer: 'It would be interesting to know to what extent those who read aloud narratives with lyric insertions differentiated their reading of narrative and lyric elements, but I have found no evidence to answer this question.'[6] The same goes for Larson, who raises similar questions about the

performance of the lyrics in Wroth's prose romance *Urania* (1621): 'Would
Wroth's readers have read or sung these lyrics silently to themselves or gathered
in a coterie setting, and prompted by the romance's depictions of poetic recitation and musical performance, might a reader have performed the song?'[7]
Only to conclude later on that 'it is not a stretch to imagine some of the readers
singing the songs embedded in the romance as part of such an event'.[8]

In the case of 17th-century Dutch prose fiction this oral and musical scen-
ario is certainly likely as well, especially because of the melody references that
have been included in the texts. These indications bring definitive evidence for
performance perhaps even closer, as they constitute a strong suggestion that
the accompanying passages were actually intended to be sung. The instructions
make the novels functional, becoming, as it were, literary–musical 'utensils',
similar to the songbooks of the time. The genres are not directly comparable,
of course, but I cannot think of any other convincing explanation for the
unusual presence of tune indications in these prose texts.

So, were the novels meant to be sung? Let us try to imagine how such a
thing would take place. First, if someone were reading a book alone, alter-
nating between silent reading and reading aloud (as the schoolmaster David
Beck did in 1624), it could well be that he or she might start singing at times.[9]
For centuries, it had been very common to sing when one was alone, so why
not while reading? We know of a farmer from the Tielerwaard who stood outside and sang in order to 'pair his voice with the sweet melody of the singing
fowl, thus praising God their benefactor, albeit as a lonely person, but with a
relieved soul'.[10] Willem Sluiter, the minister and writer from Eibergen, called
on the users of his songbook *Psalmen, lof-sangen, ende geestelike liedekens* (1661)
to sing even when they were on the road: 'If you are travelling alone on the
street, you can murmur to yourself sweetly and gently, that will shorten the
time on the road considerably. It will feel like you're in pleasant company.'[11]
Much later, in a letter from 1876, Vincent van Gogh would advise his brother
Theo to do the same: 'Do not be afraid to sing a psalm in the evening as you
walk and no one is near.'[12] Although we are perhaps less accustomed to singing
on our own in order to cheer ourselves up, to lift our spirits or to encourage
ourselves ('spoiled' as we are by modern sound devices), singing during work
or reading does seem to persist. Even today, some readers hum the songs that
they encounter in a novel.[13] On top of this, it is known that voice is not absent
even when we read quietly. Silent readers often imagine voices sounding out
the words and the muscles used for speaking move in minuscule, barely detect-
able ways as they read. 'Inner voice' is the term used to describe this phenomenon.[14] I imagine this voice could be a singing as well as a speaking one.

In the second case, if 17th-century novels were read aloud in a group, there
were several options. The most obvious is that the reader would both read and

sing, while the others listened. Another possibility is that while the reader read and sang, the group joined in. With regard to the latter option, it is a matter of speculation whether the inserted songs were sung by the listeners. On the one hand, this seems unlikely. During such joint reading sessions, there was usually only one book available, and the listeners knew many melodies but not necessarily the new lyrics, although it would obviously have been possible to hum along with the reader. On the other hand, perhaps, after all, collective singing is a possibility. It has been suggested that the fragmentary and incoherent nature of the early prose tests indicates 'a fragmented consumption'.[15] If such was indeed the case – if there were no long pieces of text read at a time, but only smaller passages – then, in principle, people would also have time to learn new lyrics together. This would be facilitated by the fact that the melodies were known to nearly everyone, and so the attention could be devoted entirely to the lyrics.

Singing, combined with singing along, was apparently not too difficult to do, and learning new melodies was expected at the time, as evidenced, for instance, in the songbook *De gheestelijcke tortelduyve* (1648) by Gabriel van Antwerpen:

Dear reader, although only some of these songs, and not all of them, contain the usual or worldly melodies to be sung (because we were unable to find a match for all of them), those who are not familiar with the music will nevertheless easily be able to learn them upon hearing them sung once or twice by someone who is more experienced musically.[16]

The same could have been true of learning new lyrics. One possibility might have involved presentation and imitation, with the reader acting as a lead singer, singing together from novels in the same way that congregations sang together at church every Sunday. Perhaps the singing from novels was like church singing as well. For example, it could have taken place according to the processes of 'lining-out' or 'hymn lining', also referred to as 'precenting the line', in which the lead singer reads or sings a line of a psalm or song, and the church congregation repeats the same line in song.[17] It is a tried and tested method that is still found in African American congregations, although it originally dates back to early European practices. Its use was officially determined by the Westminster Assembly in 1644 for all English churches ('for the present, where many in the congregation cannot read'). The same antiphonic singing style would also have been applied in the Netherlands.[18] It is reminiscent of call and response, even though it is not entirely the same: 'Lining-out involved textual repetition, whereas call-and-response typically involved a textual shift, often around a question and answer.'[19]

Figure 20. Listeners huddled around a reader in Danckertsz's *Nutte Tijdt-quistingh,* 1640. Amsterdam: Cornelis Danckertsz (detail title page). Engraving. Allard Pierson, Universiteit van Amsterdam. OK 62-6691.

The practices involving the literal repetition of a song line are reminiscent of the vocal practices in Protestant churches. They also resemble the group entertainments described in some song and emblem books, which were a popular pastime for parents and children until well into the 19th century. For example, a well-known book for recreation from 1866 describes a game in which a group of children had to listen attentively to a lead singer. The singing and repetition had evolved into a playful form of singing along that required memory and cooperation:

> The lead singer creates a circle around himself and then starts singing a song aloud. This song must be sung by all *at the same time as the lead singer:* if he remains silent, no one else should be singing either. It often happens that the lead singer stops in the middle of a line or even in the middle of a word, and those who are still singing at that moment have to offer something or pay a penalty. A folk melody that is well known and easy to sing lends itself best as the song for the lead singer.[20]

This game would have appealed to the readers of the Golden Age, who also loved such pleasant and surprising forms of entertainment. For example, consider the 'soete spelletjes, raetseltjes en het speelen en singhen' ('sweet games, riddles, full of playing and singing') of Danckertsz's characters in the *Nutte Tijdt-quistingh der Amstelsche Jonckheyt* (1640), not to mention the explicit reference to 'a circle' for their joint reading session:

> Meanwhile, Melibea and Lucretia were already busy with the book; they were reading the assignment. This prompted the Queen, who noticed this, to ask Constantine, who was busy praying, if he would read it aloud, partly because it was his turn to entertain the company by presenting something. They all now took their places, formed a circle and, after Constantine received the book from Lucretia, he began to read as follows.[21]

Was this fiction or reality? The two were probably a lot closer than we might be inclined to think today.

Figure 21. Joachim Wtewael, *Portrait of Johan Wtewael*, 1628. Oil on panel. Centraal Museum Utrecht 18021.

10

CONCLUSION

Although many questions remain, this initial exploratory study into music in the prose fiction of the 17th century has brought to light significant new information.

As I stated at the beginning, like every researcher dealing with this material, I encountered the problem that 17th-century prose texts are in many ways different from the novels of today and, unfortunately, there is no comprehensive survey of the genre in the early modern period, particularly when it comes to the Netherlands. The fragmentary structure of many of the texts runs counter to our current idea of what a novel should be, and the mixing of genres arouses resistance and a sense of strangeness (although numerous 'hybrid' novels are currently being published, providing a counterweight to such resistance). In addition, one reason for the relative paucity of research into the subject may be that there were no generally accepted regulations governing the writing of early prose fiction. Although the omission has been rectified quite well elsewhere in Europe, such is not yet the case for the Netherlands – despite previous findings and repeated calls from literary historians to look more closely at the nature and development of early Dutch prose fiction.

One purpose of this study was to respond to such calls. To this end, the incorporation of music within the prose texts provides an effective means of access to the larger domain of literary history, and my specific focus can therefore widen out to some further, general issues. The same undoubtedly applies to research into one of the other inserted genres, discussed before. Particular attention should, of course, be paid to the 'dialogic' character of early modern Dutch prose fiction – to use Bakhtin's term again – which means that further research into the ways in which all these incorporated elements relate to the surrounding prose is called for.

As we have seen, music is abundantly present in prose fiction, and its influence is considerable. In more than two-thirds of the analysed corpus, music plays a role in one way or another, often thematically, but also in structural ways. Music is discussed by the characters, and they are defined by their love of or sensitivity to it. As in contemporary stage plays, one of the most important functions of music in prose fiction is that of characterisation. Furthermore, within the storytelling world, music often acts as a catalyst for emotions, in some cases leading to intense physical reactions. Several stereotypical musical situations can additionally be identified, such as the overhearing of songs, solitary lamentations, serenades and wooing scenes. Songs (and lyrical passages in general) add an extra dimension to the content of the novel. They allowed for self-expression – strong emotions found their vent in song rather than in prose.[1] They provide moments that might compensate for the lack of psychological depth for which later researchers have sometimes reproached the early novelists. As many adventures come to a halt, the characters stand back to consider their fate, and the reader/listener gains some insight into their inner life (an effect that is frequently deepened by way of inserted letters or, for instance, poetry carved into trees).[2] Thus, the song-insets were also a constructive element in the narration: they function as a narrative device that can accelerate, retard or freeze the story.[3] Musical moments did influence, in other words, both content and structure of the prose work as a whole. Further research is needed in order to determine in more detail how musical elements were deployed in different types of prose texts and what affective impact they might have had, and to explore how all this 'literary music' developed throughout the century.

Studying the function of music in 17th-century prose fiction was in itself a sufficiently demanding topic, but my discovery that Dutch novelists began mentioning tune indications in their prose texts led me to pay attention also to the way novels were read at that time. After all, the intriguing phenomenon of inserting titles of melodies is difficult to understand from within the texts themselves. It is for that reason, amongst others, that I do not agree with Pierre Dubois, who claims that in the early modern novel 'the question of sound is less central and music matters in it primarily as a topos'.[4] In search of a more satisfactory explanation, I discovered that the contexts within which the prose texts functioned were of decisive importance. The reading of novels was not necessarily silent, even though there was silent communication between author and reader in the 17th century to a much greater degree than in the centuries before. Nevertheless, reading aloud was still a widespread practice. In other words, 'the neutral world of the eye' had not yet replaced 'the magical world of the ear'.[5] On the contrary, the latter one dictated people's experience of literature – as the many recent studies on the musical, vocal and oral dimensions of the early modern period reveal. Books were not objects for quiet, solitary use in the first place. Reading was, for most people, still a fundamentally social act. Once we understand this, many pieces of the puzzle fall into place.

For example, the hybridity that is a central characteristic of 17th-century prose fiction did not arise from incompetence but from a different general orientation. Books not only functioned as material objects; they were also 'live events', or even 'immersive experiences'.[6] A main purpose of prose fiction publications was to stimulate oral performance and in doing so keep a listening and reading audience captivated. Musical elements and other inserted genres (e.g. poetry, sayings, letters and illustrations) served this goal. They were there primarily for the reader, and not for the writer. Everything was used to entertain and move people, because *varietas delectat*. Unlike many writers from around 1900, novelists of the 17th century did not regard music as an 'ideal art' after which they tried to model their writings. Music was used instead in a very practical and functional way, serving as one of the means by which writers captured the attention of their audiences.

Such a practical purpose is likely to have applied also to the melodies that were inserted into novels. It was with good reason that melodies were explicitly mentioned with the songs: they were obviously intended to be sung on the spot by the reader of the novel. Or otherwise, the tunes were at least meant to resound in the heads of silent readers. For us modern readers, who 'have learned not to listen', this may feel rather uncomfortable – considering that until recently even ballads on broadsides and songs in poetry collections and stage plays have tended to be read silently.[7] However, such performance awareness is necessary, in order to fully appreciate the dimensions of the texts discussed here.

This study provides a new perspective on the historical development of prose fiction, while also generating unexpected insight into reading behaviour at the time. In this way fiction can be a fruitful source for reflecting on reality. As observed by Albert Mancini in his commentary on early modern Italian prose: 'The novel reflects, perhaps better than other genres, the ideological, ethical and literary climate of seventeenth-century society. Novelists were dependent upon the approval of a wide public and they therefore consciously reflected the ideas and tastes generally held.'[8] The fact that Dutch prose fiction seems to distinguish itself internationally by the use of melody indications indicates that writers in the Netherlands closely followed the tastes of their readers, whose preferences they respected in deciding which musical elements to incorporate in their texts. As Marguerite Yourcenar wrote about the anonymous proofreader at the 17th-century Amsterdam printing house of Elias Adriaensen, in her novella *Un homme obscur. La vie et la mort de Nathanaël, dans la Hollande du XVIIè siècle* (1985), 'This man was humming poems by Anacreon in Greek as he worked, which he adapted to popular tunes of his time.'[9] The use of one's own, individually selected melodies was a well-tried method. Novelists in the Netherlands took advantage of it eagerly, pandering to the vocal successes that circulated widely, in people's houses, on the streets – thanks also to the wealth of songbooks and verse miscellanies. Together, all of these aspects confirm the specific musical character of the Dutch novel at the time.

NOTES

1 INTRODUCTION

1 See e.g. Albert, 'A Bibliography of Jazz Fiction'; Brown, *An Annotated Bibliography*; Gibbs, *Music Fiction*.

2 Cf. Rippl, *Handbook of Intermediality*, and e.g. Wolf, *The Musicalization of Fiction*; Wolf, 'Musicalized Fiction and Intermediality', Wolf, 'Literature and Music'. I leave the problematic nature of the term 'intermediality' out of consideration here. See also Bernhart, Scher and Wolf, *Word and Music Studies: Defining the Field*: the first publication of the International Association for Word and Music Studies (WMA), which was founded in 1997 to promote transdisciplinary scholarly inquiry devoted to the relations between literature, verbal texts, and language and music.

3 Clements, *Virginia Woolf: Music, Sound, Language*, especially chapter 6, 189–226: 'The performativity of language: *The Waves* musicalized.'

4 Smyth, *Music in Contemporary British Fiction*, 7.

5 For instance, in treatises on the hierarchy within the arts. Subordinate in the sense of dependent. Music was not an independent art, for a long time it only existed in connection with (one of) the other art disciplines. Settings of words, for example, were granted a higher status than merely instrumental works. At the same time, music was one of the core disciplines of a humanist education, and also the influential Pythagorean conception of 'the music of the spheres' or 'musica universalis' (of which our 'real' music on earth was a reflection or imitation) gives evidence of the great importance that was attached to music.

6 See e.g. Aronson, *Music and the Novel*; Petermann, *The Musical Novel*; Smyth, *Music in Contemporary British Fiction*.

7 See e.g. Wolf, *The Musicalization of Fiction*. Cf. also the British Academy multidisciplinary conference *Song in the Novel*, organised by Jennifer Rushworth, Barry Ife and Hannah Scott, which took place on 30 September and 1 October 2021 (unfortunately, just after I submitted the manuscript of this book).

2 MUSIC IN THE NOVEL BEFORE 1900

1 I also wrote a study on the influence of music on painting during this period, particularly with regard to the work of Vincent van Gogh: Veldhorst, *Van Gogh & Music. Symphony in Blue and Yellow*.

2 Veldhorst, *De perfecte verleiding*; Veldhorst, *Zingend door het leven*.

3   Cf. Rubery, *The Untold Story*, 20: 'poetry recitations have not suffered the same crit-
     ical neglect as prose ones'. Richards, *Voices and Books*, 24, focuses on renaissance prose
     narrations, which are not instant 'recognizable oral texts'. Larson, *The Matter of Song*,
     207, points at 'the musicality of seemingly "non-theatrical" genres such as the sonnet
     sequence and the romance'.

4   Richards, *Voices and Books*, 249: 'the mode of writing we have come to associate with
     the shift to thoughtful silent reading'.

5   More specifically: Elias, 'Musical Performance' (about Italy, 16th century); Garke,
     The Use of Songs (England, 16th century); Tucker, 'Une autre de vostre ventre' (France,
     17th century); Chapter 3 'Voicing Lyric' in Larson, *The Matter of Song* (England, 17th
     century); Freedman, *Laurence Sterne*; Hocutt, 'Music and Rhetoric' (England, 18th
     century); Dubois, *Music in the Georgian Novel* (England, 18th century); Noske, 'Sound
     and Sentiment' (England, 18th and 19th century). Relatively more research has been
     done on music in French medieval prose, see e.g. Boulton, *The Song in the Story*.

6   Garke, *The Use of Songs*, 6.

7   Gasta, 'Writing to be Heard', 88. Gasta did rely on a number of previous Spanish-lan-
     guage publications. In an earlier article he pointed out the importance of music in *Don
     Quixote*: 'Throughout Don Quijote a rather considerable number and variety of lyrical
     poems appear frequently, and they are regularly accompanied by an abundance and
     diversity of period instruments. Moreover, the novel also boasts references to pieces
     and instruments that appear as contextual information, and entire themes or episodes
     in the novel often turn upon the fusion of song, dance, and instrumentalism.' Gasta,
     'Señora, donde hay música', 357.

8   Dubois, *Music in the Georgian Novel*, 2.

9   I have previously drawn attention to the potential of this research area: Veldhorst,
     'Pharmacy for the Body and Soul', 238; Veldhorst, 'Vergilius' Bucolica op muziek', 32.

10   Mancini, 'Narrative Prose', 318. He mentions this number with regard to the situation
     in Italy. By comparison, he mentions Dante's *Divine Comedy*, which was reprinted only
     three times in the same period (1600–1699).

11   Quoted in Mancini, 'Narrative Prose', 318. Characterisation of Nolfi's text as 'curioso
     antiromanzo' in Battistelli, 'Nolfi, Vincenzo'.

12   Moreau, 'Seventeenth-Century Fiction in the Making', 1.

13   I follow Moreau, 'Seventeenth-Century Fiction in the Making', 1: 'It is our conviction
     that prose fiction is better understood when considered as a trans-European phenom-
     enon.' Interestingly, many foreign novels were published in Amsterdam at the time.
     For a French example, see Glomski and Moreau, *Seventeenth-Century Fiction*, 187.

3 PROBLEMS STUDYING THE EARLY MODERN NOVEL

1   Frow, *Genre*, 145.

2   Leemans, *Het woord is aan de onderkant*, 34: 'There is no history of the Dutch novel
     and, as Pol claimed in his 1987 study […] it will be a while before it can be written.'
     Koppenol, 'Zoveel jeu en toch niet te lezen', agreed in 2006: 'We are still not much
     further along than the stage of gathering bibliographic information, a few introduc-
     tory and exploratory articles, and some (facsimile) editions.'

3   See e.g. Pavel, *The Lives of the Novel*; Solbach, 'Early Modern German Narrative Prose';
     Moore, *The Novel*; Keymer, *Prose Fiction in English*.

4   Van Gemert, 'Stenen in het mozaïek', 21.

5   ''t Is met de welsprekendheid als met het water, 't welk het beste is als het zuiver, licht en minst smaak heeft. 't Is een subtiele kunst, geen kunst te gebruiken.' In his *Banket-werk van Goede gedachten*, part I (1657), 198. Quoted in Jansen, 'Johan de Brune en de stijldeugden', 79. Ovid, *Ars amatoria*, 2: 313.

6   'De stijl is even, en natuyrlyck; de begrijpinghen zijn er klaer en onvermenght beworpen; kort, de schoonste kunst die haer bekleed, is, dat sy 'er naeckt van is.' In his popular letter instruction booklet (which enjoyed popularity in the Netherlands as well): *Fatsoenlycke send-briefschryver* (1651), 462. Quoted in Porteman, 'J'ay pris pour duppes tous les Pays-Bas', 229.

7   Finkelstein and McCleery, *An Introduction to Book History*, 112.

8   'de zonderlingste gewrochten die eene breidelooze verbeelding heeft kunnen scheppen'. Te Winkel, *De ontwikkelingsgang*, 302.

9   Quoted in Koppenol, 'Zoveel jeu en toch niet te lezen', 43.

10 Grootes, 'Een zeeheld op vrijersvoeten', 315.

11 Leemans, *Het woord is aan de onderkant*, 61: 'by not interpreting possible divergent choices as inability, unwillingness, or lack of genius of the author, but to take these choices seriously and investigate why one chose their own path'.

12 See Koppenol, 'Zoveel jeu en toch niet te lezen', 43.

13 Cf. listening to atonal music: it requires a different attitude in the same way – no 'plot' (tonal centre) either, which causes the listener to lack a sense of direction. It also causes similar irritations ('unlistenable').

14 Koppenol, 'Zoveel jeu en toch niet te lezen', 44.

15 Cf. also Brouwer, 'Rondom het boek', 88: 'Mentions of reading aloud in literature are rather anecdotal. The phenomenon deserves more systematic research, in which material factors, forms and sociability, levels of literacy, and cultural mediators deserve attention.'

16 Richards, *Voices and Books*, resp. 2 and 283. Her book was connected to a broader initiative led by Richards and Richard Wistreich, 'Voices and Books, 1500–1800', which elucidated the orality and aurality of early modern reading.

17 Larson, *The Matter of Song*, 207.

18 Marsh, 'The Sound of Print', 173. One might think Marsh's phrase inspired the title of my essay. Surprisingly, however, this was not the case.

19 Vitz, *Orality and Performance*, text on back cover.

20 See among others Griffith, 'Performative Reading', 103.

21 Vitz, Regalado and Lawrence, *Performing Medieval Narrative*, 5.

22 Kundera, *The Art of the Novel*.

23 Kundera, *Testaments Betrayed*, part 3, speaks of 'caesuras, or halftime breaks' in history. He distinguishes between literary and musical compositions from the 'first half' (i.e. until the 19th century) and those from the 'second half' (i.e. from the 19th century onwards).

24 Woolf, 'The Countess of Pembroke's Arcadia', 49.

25 Pavel, *The Lives of the Novel*, 16.

26 Pavel, *The Lives of the Novel*, 6.

27 Pavel, *The Lives of the Novel*, 7.

28 Cf. Moreau, 'Seventeenth-Century Fiction in the Making', 15 (note 78).

29 Koopmans and Verhuyck, *Een kijk op anekdotencollecties*, 53.

30 Koopmans and Verhuyck, *Een kijk op anekdotencollecties*, 53.

31   Resp. Bakhtin, *The Dialogic Imagination*, 320; Solbach, 'Early Modern German Narrative Prose', 469.

4 MUSIC AS AN INSERTED GENRE

1   Bakhtin, *The Dialogic Imagination*, 320.
2   Braund, 'Prosimetrum'.
3   See on this habit also Larson, *The Matter of Song*, 125 (esp. note 58).
4   Grootes, 'Een zeeheld op vrijersvoeten', 313 and 309 resp.
5   Solbach, 'Early Modern German Narrative Prose', 503 (note 46).
6   Curtius, *European Literature and the Latin Middle Ages*, 152.
7   Cf. 'A short cut to the heart.' Watt, *The Rise of the Novel*, 191–95. Flaubert's phrasing is in a letter to Louise Colet (7 July 1853).
8   Martin, 'L'Illustration de *L'Astrée*', 235. See also Ionescu, *Book Illustration in the Long Eighteenth Century*, 17.
9   Omeis, *Gründliche Anleitung*, 218.
10   Von Birken, *Teutsche Rede-, Bind- und Dichtkunst*. Cf. Solbach, 'Early Modern German Narrative Prose', 484.
11   ''t Geen men eigentlijk Romans noemd, zijn verzieringen van Minne-handelingen geschreeven in Prose met konst, tot vermaak en onderwijzing der Leezere.' Quotation from the translation of Van Broekhuizen from 1679. Pol, *Romanbeschouwing in voorredes*, 60.
12   Cf. Boulton, *The Song in the Story*, 26 et seq.
13   'volgens zekere regelen geschreeven zijn, vermits het anders een verwarde vergadering zonder order, en zonder fraayigheid zoude weezen'. Pol, *Romanbeschouwing in voorredes*, 60.
14   Pol, *Romanbeschouwing in voorredes*, 61 (note 13).
15   Schlegel, *Gespräch über die Poesie*, 336. Cf. the afterword of H. Eichner, 10: 'Der Roman ist das volkommene Mischgedicht.'
16   Thus, to him the remark by Bakhtin, *The Dialogic Imagination*, 322 applied: 'The Romantics considered the presence of verses in the novel one of its constitutive features.' See also Ryan, 'Hybrid Forms in German Romanticism', 180.

5 MUSIC IN 17TH-CENTURY DUTCH PROSE FICTION

1   For this list, I used Buisman, *Populaire prozaschrijvers*, who, from all available bibliographies, applies the least stringent selection criteria and therefore provides the most comprehensive overview. I have supplemented this by data from Pol, *Romanbeschouwing in voorredes*; and Porteman and Smits-Veldt, *Een nieuw vaderland voor de muzen*.
2   The proportion of original Dutch prose is small – most texts are translations – although the boundary between the two is not always clear, as many translations are in fact loose adaptations.
3   Most of the texts are available in digital form, which made this method feasible. The following terms were used: *muziek, lied, deun, zingen, zingt, zang, geluid, stem, toon, klank, instrument, luit, viool, trompet, trom, harp, citer, fluit* and *dans*. Different spellings were used for each term (e.g. *muziek* and *musijck*).

4   Wolf designed a scheme in which the usage of music is divided into thematisation ('telling') and 'imitation' ('showing'), with further subdivision into 'positional', 'referential' and 'technical forms'. Wolf, 'Musicalized Fiction and Intermediality', 52. Later he further adapted and nuanced his analytical model. See Wolf, 'Literature and Music', 468.

5   The quantities mentioned are an estimate. The categories are not easy to define; the reality is too complex for that.

6   In some texts, however, a separate song attachment (with tune indications) has been added, often in close thematic relationship with the main text. Remarkably, this often concerns prose texts written for and/or about women. For instance, *Spiegel der quade vrouwen* (1644): the main text has no songs, but the short stories that were added to it do. The prose dialogue *Het net der wellustigheyt* (1646) has only one song. However, the main text is followed by an annex containing 13 'Uytgelese Minnezangen' ('Exquisite Love Songs') including melody indications. The same is true of *Schoole voor de jonge dochters* (1658), which has a supplement containing 11 'Minnezangen'.

7   Hart, *Cervantes' Exemplary Fictions*, 78: 'The song is found in several contemporary collections and survives today in the oral traditions of several Spanish provinces.' Hart also includes the text of the song, as well as the English translation: 'Mother, you have guards to watch me, but if I don't guard myself, no one else can guard me.'

8   'Ey moeder wat gaet u dogh aen, / Dat ghy my dus besluyt? / Wat hoeft hier soo veel wacht te staen, / Seght my wat dit beduyt. / Wat baet grendel of slot, / Het is maer enkel spot. / Eylaes, eylaes. / De min en wil niet zijn, / Soo bedwonghen met veel pijn. / Die bemint die wil vry zijn.' Cervantes, *Den ialoerssen Carrizale*, 66–67. In the Dutch translation, the song has two verses. The melody used is 'Bellissima Mirtilla', the incipit of one of the five-part *Balletti* (1591) by Gian Giacomo Gastoldi ('La Bellezza').

9   Cf. Boutcher, 'Transnational Cervantes', 108: 'the *Novelas ejemplares*, published at Madrid in 1613, were translated by de Rosset and d'Audiguier and issued by Jean Richer at Paris in 1614–15. […] This French version was in turn translated into Dutch, German, and Italian.'

10 *Les nouvelles de Miquel de Cervantes*, 150: 'Que vous sert-il ma bonne Mère / De m'enfermer dans une Tour, / Et qu'en une prison austere / Les Gardes veillent nuict & iour: Il n'est n'y garden y closure / Qui puisse empescher la Nature / Lors qu'elle veut faire l'Amour.'

11 The latter contains at least three strophic passages in italics, although it is not certain that all three were meant to be sung.

12 Although some scholars doubt whether his text can be called a novel, given its many educational digressions. Samuel van Hoogstraten's *Schone Rooseliin* (1650) would then be more eligible. Cf. Weststeijn, 'Samuel van Hoogstraten', 186 and 183.

13 Spies and Frijhoff, *Hard-Won Unity*, 582. The literature historian Jan te Winkel speaks of a series of Arcadian frame narratives that would be worth studying. See Weststeijn, 'Samuel van Hoogstraten', 198.

14 'Indien sy desen voorslagh een mael willen beginnen in 't werck te stellen, sullen wy haer de Deure voor de neuse toe sluyten; ende soo sy ons komen besoecken, sullen wy haer het Franse Liedtje van Montelimar te vooren singhen: op de wijse, Blijft daer buyten, Snode Guyten: want anders sou de Duyvel veel eerder by de Kalveren als by de Koeyen zijn.' Quevedo, *Seven wonderlijcke ghesichten*, 31. Cf. Moser, 'Overdroomde dromen', 54.

15 Worp, *Briefwisseling van Constantijn Huygens*, letter 2264 and 2275, Joan van Brosterhuysen to Constantijn Huygens, 18 October and 22 November 1639 resp. See also Van Seters, 'De Nederlandse uitgaven van *The Man in the Moone*.'

16 'Die geen ghemeenschap en heeft met eenige andere Tael die ick oyt hoorde [...] om datse soo seer niet bestaet in woorden en letteren als in toonen; een rouw gheluydt dat men door gheen letteren kan uytdrucken.' Godwin, *Het rechte eerste Deel van de Man in de Maen*, 85–86.

17 Godwin, *The Man in the Moone*, 108.

18 'Lunar language' refers to a tonal language, like Chinese. See William Poole's introduction to Godwin, *The Man in the Moone*, 44–46. Cf. 'Oceanic language' in Melville's *Moby Dick* (1851), which is an associative instead of syntagmatic language (Packham, 'Pip's Oceanic Voice', 570–71). See also with regard to Woolf's *The Waves* (1931): 'creating the smooth flow and effect of undulation in the language' (Clements, *Virginia Woolf: Music, Sound, Language*, 193). Lunar language, oceanic language, wavy language: semantics coincides with form in these novels.

19 Sels, *Zedelyke uitspanningen*, 12–16. The page with musical notation is included between 12–13. It is a melody with a figured bass line. Many thanks to Riet Schenkeveld-van der Dussen, who drew my attention to this fine example.

20 'Ik hoope, dat het gezang den leezer niet mishagen zal, en daarom deel ik hem hetzelve, zo onopgetoid, als het is, en in diervoegen als het Sincerus paste, gulhartig mede.' Sels, *Zedelyke uitspanningen*, 11. Sincerus is one of the characters.

21 'In dezen landstreek heeft men geene drukpersse, ten minsten niet dan op eenen zeer wyden afstand. Een myner vrienden, te Amsterdam woonende, (en dezen heb ik ook het gezang en het grafschrift te danken,) nam de bestelling over het drukken op zich; door wien dan ook deze vier geschiedenissen den dag zien, in de welken zy, door twee voornaame Meesteren in Plaatsnykunde en Zangkunst opgetoid, als voorwerpen verschynen, die zich gaerne wilden aangezien hebben als te gering voor den nydt en te ernstig voor den laster, en wel in 't byzonder als zodanigen, die, voor mynen eenvouwigen land- en buurman opgesteld, alleenelyk, by mangel van drukpersse, zich in eene der grootste en voornaamste handeldryvende steden van ons Vaderland, voor het oog van verheven en spitsvondige geesten vertoonen.' Sels, *Zedelyke uitspanningen*, *7v–*8r.

6 FUNCTIONS OF MUSIC IN 17TH-CENTURY DUTCH PROSE

1 Wolf, 'Musicalized Fiction and Intermediality', 52; Wolf, 'Literature and Music', 468.

2 'Een trommel oft trompet hoorde hy veel liever dan eenen Psalm zinghen, ende scheen alleenlijc gheboren te zyn tot zuypen ende bloetvergieten.' Balde, *Den Lust-Hof*, 114.

3 'O spitsbroeders, wie mag die jonkvrouw of Goddin zijn die het groot gewelf bearbeit en zo aangenaam zingt dat het gehele huis daerop weêrgalmt?' Homerus, *De Dooling van Ulisses*, 191.

4 'Zy gingen al zingende voor, malkander by de hand houdende, zo datze bequamelijk konden danzen.' Heliodorus, *De getrouwe liefde*, 106.

5 The zither is a precursor of the guitar. In Cervantes, *Den ialoerssen Carrizale*, 36, 'guitar' is translated as 'Quinteerne'.

6 'Dese Boogsnoer (om in 't kort te seggen) was een Instrument, waer op Andronicus veel pleeghde te slaen, en daer mede Musijck en vrolijckheyt hem selver toe te speelen,

noemende deselve (spotsghewijse) sijne Remedie voor allerleye Sieckten.' Fuller, *Andronicus*, 62. Probably not a real musical instrument ('bow string': actually, hunting arrow).

7   'Klim-op trock'er schoenen uyt, en begost'er wacker op te speelen; Win-al nam een nieuwe palmen-beesem, diese by gheval vondt, en begost'er mede al sleepende een schor geluyt te geven, 't welck nochtans met 'et schoen-musijck overeen quam: Monipodio smeet een schotel stucken, en stack twee van de scherven, als klepperbeentjes, tusschen sijn vingers, en begonder seer meesterlick op te speelen, onder de Bas en Tenor van de schoen en besem.' Cervantes, *Monipodios Hol*, 52.

8   'Dat mij Meesters Juffer in een boeck placht te lesen, wanneer ick in haer huys verkeerde, het welck anders niet handelde als van Herders en Herderinnen, en seyde datse haer gantsche leven al singende en spelende op Sackpijpen, Violen, Rinckeltuych, Ruyspijpen, en andere vreemde instrumenten, doorbrachten. Ick luysterde somtijds nae haer woorden, en hoorde hoese las, dat de herder Amfrisius soo uytnemende heerlick songh. En sijn onvergelijckelicke Belizarde tot aen de sterren verhief, ja dat'er niet een boom op de bergen van gantsch Arcadien was waer onder hy niet gesongen had, van dat de Son uyt de armen van Aurora gingh, tot dat hy in die van Thetis weder verschool, en dat selfs de nacht, die met sijn bruyne vleugels het aerdtrijck bedeckt, hem niet deden ophouden van sijn wel gesongen klaegh-liederen uyt te drucken […]. Het gedenckt my dat ick verscheyde boecken meer van dees slagh heb hooren lesen.' Cervantes, *Monipodios Hol*, 103–4.

9   'waer over sy sich niet weynich verwonderden, om dat haer docht dat dit geen plaets was, daer men sulck gesang sou mogen verwachten. Want dat men seggen wil, dat men somwijlen in Bosschen en velden Harderinnen vint, die bysonder wel singen konnen, is meer het vernemen en de vont van Rijmers, als waerheydt.' Cervantes, *Den verstandigen vroomen ridder*, chapter 27, 302–3.

10 Solbach, 'Early Modern German Narrative Prose', 499.

11 Cf. Blaak, *Geletterde levens*, 67: 'Poetry was a writing skill that not everyone possessed.' See also the pages on writing and power in Finkelstein and McCleery, *An Introduction to Book History*, 38–42.

12 Cf. Solbach, 'Early Modern German Narrative Prose', 478, about a character in Jorg Wickram's *Der Goldtfaden*: 'His beautiful singing voice and noble bearing signify his exceptional character.'

13 'als het geluid der zwanen, of zoodanige andere vogels, en het geruisch der westewinden en waterbeken'. Tasso, *Het Verloste Jeruzalem*, 565 and 636 resp.

14 'Zy vielen met menigte overhoop, en d'een belette d'ander. Enige verloren in zo groot een gedrang het leven, terwijl d'andere van de stellingen, en uyt de vensteren zich te barsten sprongen. Veel braken hals en armen. Enige lagen 'er dood, en andere verlemt. 't Zuchten en schreeuwen, met knarssen en breken verzelt, steeg tot in den Hemel. 't Vervaert gespuys, keerde snellijk om, van wat zijde 't geluyt der Horen quam.' Ariosto, *De razende Roelant*, 344.

15 'One of the most common pastoral scenes' is mentioned by Pavel, *The Lives of the Novel*, 96: 'An Arcadian walking in the woods, alone or with a friend, happens to hear the lonely eclogue of an unknown shepherd. The passers-by lend the song a friendly ear, inquire about the singer's sorrows, and offer to help. The singer tells his or her story, offering a narrative to explain the background to the lyrical passages.'

16 'Hy troosten sijn vrient, soo hy best kon, belovende sijn best te doen, en onderwijlen besich zijnde met sijn eyge vryery te vertellen, en met een lijdtsaam opset Rooselijn te beschuldigen, vernamen sy (schoon de Nachtegaal 't geboomt' als Orgelpijpen dé klinken)

een die, al singende, beneên aan de beek bleef staan.' Van Hoogstraten, *Schone Rooseliin*, 108. The passage is followed by a song (four verses, beginning with the line 'Soete Nimph mijn schoone Hageroos!' to the melody of 'Als Garint sijn ooghjes open dé').

17   'gelijk de doorluchtige Poëet *Hooft* door sijn *Dorilea* seyt. […]. Wanneer de hovelingen / Een vrolijk Lietje singen, / 't En is van vreugde niet, / Maar 't is, om het verdriet / Daar 't hart af wort gebeten, / Een weynigh te vergeten.' Van Hoogstraten, *Schone Rooseliin*, 110. Cf. Hooft, *Granida*, 51 (the words of Dorilea at the end of the first act).

18   Thomas, *Music and the Origins of Language*, 156.

19   'de galm van een Citer zo lieffelijk in de oore, dat het hart van Narsisa daer door werdt ingenomen, en buyten zig zelven verruckt, wen ze een vermenginge van een gorgeltrant daer aldus hoort by uytboezemen'. Boekholt, *De wonderlijke vryagien*, 194. Cf. Grootes, 'Een zeeheld op vrijersvoeten', 314.

20   'divine stemme'; 'dese schoone Sonne, dewelcke op 't Instrument speelde ende so melodieuselijck songh'. De Rosset, *Waerachtige treurige gheschiedenissen*, 284–5.

21   Garke, *The Use of Songs*, 61. See also Larson, *The Matter of Song*, 126: 'overheard expostulations and dialogues, whether spoken or sung, were a frequent plot device in the period'.

22   'De buik-loop van onze Marquis, veranderde in een schielijke hardlyvigheid, wanneer hy midden in het hartje van zyn kakken zynde, een zoo aangenamen musiek in d'ooren kreeg, en hebbende wat eijeren in de pers geslagen, en de drukkery zoo kort gemaakt als 't mogelijk was, begaf hy zig na de kamer daar hy dit geluid vandaan hoorde komen.' Heinsius, *Don Clarazel de Gontarnos*, 380.

23   Thomas, *Music and the Origins of Language*, 152: 'Excessive passion was the mark of an intense sensibility.'

24   Flaherty, 'Transport, Ecstasy, and Enthusiasm', 82–83.

25   Wolf, 'Musicalized Fiction and Intermediality', 52, Wolf, 'Literature and Music', 468.

26   Wolf, 'Literature and Music', 468, labels the phenomenon as '(partial) reproduction', but that term captures only the phenomenon of inserting existing songs (combinations of texts and tunes), not that of any newly written lyrics.

27   See e.g. Marsh, *Music and Society*, 132. On contrafacts in the Amsterdam theatre: Veldhorst, *De perfecte verleiding*, 29. My impression is that contrafacts in stage plays are less often accompanied by tune indications than the song texts in prose works – an observation that requires further research.

28   On pp. 48–49, *The Jealous Estremaduran: A Novel* (London, 1709) contains a song consisting of nine numbered and italicised verses, each consisting of four lines (incipit 'Mother! Keep me not under lock and key'). A later translation, *The Jealous Estremaduran* (London, 1729), contains a very different song (pp. 271–72), with similar content, but with six italicised verses of 4, 4, 4, 6, 6 and 10 lines, respectively (incipit 'Good Mother, if you please, you may'). The last song was apparently popular; it was later sold separately as sheet music, given its mention on Amazon: '*Good Mother, if you please you may.* [Song.] Unknown Binding. Import, 1750.'

29   I borrowed data on the translations from Vogler, *Vital d'Audiguier*, but his list appears to be incomplete (e.g. he does not mention the 1663 edition that I used).

30   D'Audiguier, *Histoire trage-comique*, resp. Livre III: 'Puis qu'en fin ma belle Ypolite' (1 x 10 lines, italics). Livre IX: 'Beautez dont l'esclat nompareil' (4 x 6 lines, italics), 'Ce bois couvert d'or & d'esmail' (4 x 6 lines, italics). Livre X: 'Douce rive autrefois si verte' (5 x 4 lines, italics, entitled: 'Complainte de la rive Seine'), 'Une Nymphe sortit de l'onde' (9 x 4 lines, italics).

31   D'Audiguier, *Liebes-Beschreibung*, resp. IX. Buch: 'Schöninne, dero Strahlen' (numbered
     4 x 6 lines), 'Diese so Zierlich vergüldete Lanze' (numbered 4 x 6 lines). X. Buch: 'Süse
     Seene, die vor diesen' (4 x 7 lines, entitled 'Klagegesang auf das Ufer Seine'),
     'Unlängsten hörte ich schmerzlich flehen' (9 x 4 lines).

32   D'Audiguier, *A Tragi-Comicall History*, resp. Lib. 3: 'Hipolita fair, if in the end' (1 x 10
     lines, italics). Lib. 9: 'You beauties, whose excelling light' (4 x 6 lines, italics), 'This staff
     enameled with gold' (4 x 6 lines, italics).

33   D'Audiguier, *De treurige doch bly-eyndigende historie*, resp. III. Boeck: 'Terwijl ick Ypolite
     bederven' (numbered 2 x 8 lines, italics, melody: 'Heureux se-jour de Parthenisse'). IX.
     Boeck: 'Goddinne voor wiens stralen' (numbered 4 x 8 lines, italics, melody: 'Verdwaelde
     Coninginne'), 'Dees speer bedeckt met cierlijck gout' (numbered 4 x 6 lines, italics, no
     melody indication). IX. Boeck: 'Seyne die soo groen te vooren' (numbered 3 x 6 lines,
     italics, melody: 'Yets moet ick u Laura &c.'), 'Een stroom, Goddin, quam lest hier
     voren' (numbered 9 x 4 lines, italics, melody: 'Neri ô Schoonste &c.')

34   Blasius, *Lysander en Kaliste*, p. 63: 'Hypolite!' (3 x 10 lines, no italics, but numbered,
     melody: 'Repicavan'), p. 104: 'Beroemde Seyne van Parijs' (titled 'Eensaam gesang van
     Lysander', numbered 3 x 4 lines, italics, melody: 'Courante simple') and p. 105: 'Het
     is helaas! niet lang verleen' (numbered 3 x 10 lines, italics, melody: 'Courante la
     Bare').

35   On 17th-century Dutch song culture: Veldhorst, 'Pharmacy for the Body and
     Soul'; Veldhorst, *Zingend door het leven*. On music in the Dutch Golden Age in gen-
     eral: Veldhorst, 'Musical Life'. See also the many publications by Louis Peter Grijp,
     founder of the Dutch Song Database, which contains over 180,000 songs in Dutch
     and Flemish, from the 12th to the 20th century. Its main sources are songbooks,
     broadsides, song manuscripts and fieldwork recordings.

36   Marsh, *Music and Society*, 248.

37   Marsh, *Music and Society*, 233: 'The overwhelming majority of the ballads published in
     the early modern period named but did not note specific tunes.' Larson, *The Matter of
     Song*, 19: 'Notated settings […] represent only a fraction of the songs that were heard
     and performed in the early modern period.'

38   I use the word 'songbook' here, although 'verse miscellany' might perhaps be better.
     On the other hand: there are plenty of Dutch examples in which the two types have
     been mixed, that is: verse miscellanies that include musical notation. Songbooks 'com-
     monly featured vocal scores or lute tablature'. Verse miscellanies 'contained lyric texts
     intended for singing that were presented without accompanying notation'. Larson,
     The Matter of Song, 114. In other European countries songbooks were more prevalent,
     along with the highly popular broadsides; verse miscellanies did exist, but obviously
     not in such large numbers as in the Netherlands.

39   Cf. Marsh, *Music and Society*, 234: 'Most of the tunes cannot be reclaimed from the
     broadsides themselves and many have been lost.'

7 READING NOVELS IN THE 17TH CENTURY

1   As the 'missing link of book history': Finkelstein and McCleery, *An Introduction to Book
    History*, 100. 'A shift of focus from the text to the reader': Cavallo and Chartier, *A
    History of Reading in the West*, 224.

2   Moreau, 'Seventeenth-Century Fiction in the Making', 13.

3   Cf. De Rooy, *Een geschiedenis van het onderwijs*, 20–21.

4   Cf. Richards, *Voices and Books*, 195: '*Legere sibi*, to read to one self, usually meant *legere tacite*, to read silently [...], but this may have meant a low mumble rather than total silence.'

5   'hoorende mij eenen wijl in de Self-strijt lesen'. Blaak, *Geletterde levens*, 93–94. Blaak says that it is possible, but not certain, that Beck is reading aloud for himself from Jacob Cats's poem *Self-strijt*. It depends on whether the friend entered the room right away. He provides another example, however: the wife of the Frisian farmer Dirck Jansz, who read out loud from the Bible for herself. Beck sang a few psalms for himself on 18 January 1624, after having read in silence first.

6   'eenen streek uijt het boeck Mespris de la Cour ende uijt de Parfaite amye van A. Herroet'. The second (a poem by Antoine Héroet) was bound with the first (a book by Antonio Guevara). See Blaak, *Geletterde levens*, 83 and 93.

7   See in this respect Gasta, 'Señora, donde hay música', who asks with regard to *Don Quixote*, 'to what extent did Cervantes mean for these poems to be performed orally, not just by the novel's characters within the frame of the novel but also by the seventeenth-century implied reader who likely read the novel aloud to a group of interested listeners?' He calls this 'difficult to gauge' but points at the many episodes in the novel (see the example below) which 'show that Cervantes's intertextual public was a listening one, not unlike his readers (listeners), who, for centuries, had been orally inclined as well'. Quotations on 358, 359 and 360, resp.

8   Blaak, *Geletterde levens*, 155.

9   'Ick heb maer twee of drie van dese boecken, en dese geven my het beste leven. En dat niet alleen aen mijn, maer oock aen vele anderen. Want als het Ooghst-tijdt is komen hier op alle Heylige dagen veel Arbeytsluy by een, daer der altoos een onder is, die lesen kan, die dan een van dese boecken in sijn handen neemt, en wy daer somtijts met ons dartig rontsom geseten, hooren soo naerstigh toe, dat wy om geen andere dingen dencken. Tenminste kan ick voor my seggen, dat ick wel nacht en dagh sou luysteren, na die schrickelijcke slagen die dese Ridders malkander geven, en de vreemde avontueren die se uyt voeren. Ick van gelijcken sey de Waerdin, want ick heb mijn leven geen beter rust in huys, als wanneer mijn Man besich is met toe te luysteren, dan sal hy niet een woort kicken, daer hy anders niet en doet als knorren en morren. [...] En wat dunckter u van Dochterken? sey den Pastoor tegens de dochter van de Waert. Wat sal ick 'er veel van seggen mijn Heer, antwoorde de Deern, al-hoe-wel ick het altemael niet en versta, vind ick 'er evenwel vermaeck in, maer niet in die vreesselijcke slagen daer mijn Vader van seyt, maer wel in die droevige klachten die de Ridders doen, wanneer se van haer Meestersen zijn, die my somwijlen doen schreyen uyt medelijden.' Cervantes, *Den verstandigen vroomen ridder*, Chapter 32, 390–91.

10   Finkelstein and McCleery, *An Introduction to Book History*, 103.

11   Chartier, 'Leisure and Sociability', 109.

12   Lankhorst, 'Lezen onder het eten', 219; Manguel, *A History of Reading*, 117.

13   Chartier, 'Leisure and Sociability', 117.

14   Blaak, *Geletterde levens*, 154.

15   Manguel, *A History of Reading*, 121. Cf. Brouwer, 'Rondom het boek', 88: 'Reading aloud seems to be a phenomenon from all times and places in Europe. It takes place both at the court of Charlemagne and Frederick II, as well as at Protestant gatherings and revolutionary clubs, in family circles, among scholars and in societies, on the streets and in the coffee house.'

16   Blaak, *Geletterde levens*, 282.

17   'wy deden des morgens en 's avondts het gebedt, met vyerigen aendacht tot Godt en songhen oock een psalm voor en nae het ghebedt, want wy hadden noch eenighe

psalm-boeckjes by ons. De meeste tijdt was ick hierin voor-leser, doch daer nae, doe de voor-leser uyt de schuyt in ons boot quam, deed hy 't selver.' Bontekoe, *Journael ofte gedenckwaerdige beschrijvinghe*, 54.

18 Manguel, *A History of Reading*, 113.

19 Finkelstein and McCleery, *An Introduction to Book History*, 101.

20 Der Weduwen, 'The Politics of Print', 152: 'The Dutch Republic was home to the most bookish, educated and literate population of early modern Europe. By the middle of the seventeenth century, literacy rates in the urban centres of the Dutch Republic reached up to 70% for men and 40% for women.' Cf. also Finkelstein and McCleery, *An Introduction to Book History*, resp. 224 and 228.

21 Finkelstein and McCleery, *An Introduction to Book History*, 103; Cavallo and Chartier, *The Cultural Uses of Print*, 276–77.

22 Fox, *Oral and Literate Culture in England*, 37.

23 Cavallo and Chartier, *A History of Reading in the West*, 224. Cf. Chartier, *The Cultural Uses of Print*, 228: 'Pictures and texts of the latter half of the 18th century implicitly contrapose the silent reading practices by city dwellers and notables and the reading aloud (for others, but for oneself as well) of the people and the peasants.'

24 As Abigail Williams has demonstrated in her study on shared reading and the elocution industry in 18th-century England: Williams, *The Social Life of Books*.

25 Rubery, *The Untold Story*.

26 See e.g. Richards, *Voices and Books*, 2: 'Reading aloud remained popular even among those who were able silent readers.'

27 Du Camp, *Souvenirs littéraires*: 'La lecture dura trente-deux heures; pendant quatre jours il lut, sans désemparer, de midi à quatre heures, de huit heures à minuit' (313); 'Nous pensons qu'il faut jeter cela au feu et n'en jamais reparler' (315).

28 Chartier, 'Leisure and Sociability', 104: reading aloud encouraged 'convivial social relations'.

29 Blaak, *Geletterde levens*, 70 and 93.

30 Specifically on 7 March 1624 during a stroll: 'I gave Breckerfelt a summary (at his request) of all the content in *Historie des Moorenlantschen geschiedenisse* on the way to shorten the time, as described and printed by Heliodorus' ('vertelde ick Breckerfelt (op zijn begeeren) onderwegs om de tijd te korten den gantschen inhout in het kort van de *Historie des Moorenlantschen geschiedenisse*, beschreven ende gedruckt door Heliodorum'). In addition, on 4 November, with Breckerfelt and his brother-in-law: he 'told him (because they insisted) the whole history of the knight Mendoza and the Duchess of Savoy from the *Clagelycke geschiedenissen* by Bandello' ('vertelde hem (op hun aenhouden) de geheele historie van de ridder Mendozza ende de hertoginnen van Savoyen uyt de *Clagelycke geschiedenissen* van Bandel'). See Blaak 2004, 93. The Dutch translation of Heliodorus appeared in 1610 in Amsterdam. The translation of Matteo Bandello was published in seven parts between 1598 and 1615 in Antwerp and Rotterdam.

31 Chartier, 'Leisure and Sociability', 114–15.

32 Chartier, *The Cultural Uses of Print*, 231.

33 Cavallo and Chartier, *A History of Reading in the West*, 74.

34 Manguel, *A History of Reading*, 250.

35 Chartier, 'Leisure and Sociability', 104.

36 Cavallo and Chartier, *A History of Reading in the West*, 63. Cf. Gasta, 'Señora, donde hay música', 359: 'As Parr makes clear, Cervantes's constant employment of verbs like *decir* and *contar* indicates that the written is a visual vehicle for oral production.'

37 Hocutt, 'Music and Rhetoric in *Tristram Shandy*', 15.
38 Woolf, *Reading History in Early Modern England*, 82.
39 Larson, *The Matter of Song*, 5, lists publications by scholars who did vital work in this field (i.e. Linda Phyllis Austern, Bonnie Gordon, Rebecca Herrisone, Richard Leppert, Christopher Marsh).
40 Richards, *Voices and Books*, 16.
41 Marsh, *Music and Society*, 256. Quote within quote: George Puttenham, *The Arte of English Poesie* (1589).
42 Richards, *Voices and Books*, 16.
43 Larson, *The Matter of Song*, 11.
44 'De meeste menschen lezen zo slegt, dat men zich moet bedroeven als men dat hoort. Lieden, vooral de Poëten, die wel, – die schoon schryven, lezen ons hunne Vaerzen zo armhartig voor, dat een mensch het zynen ergsten vyand waarlyk niet zoude wenschen. De Lectuur zet Stukjes van deezen aart onnoemelyke bevalligheden by, of ontluistert ze ten eenenmaal. Wy geven die aan de goede Gemeente, en de goede gemeente leest doorgaans zo allerelendigst als die schoolmeester, die haar, het weinige dat hy zelf wist, nog zeer onvolkomen leèrde. Elk mensch heeft, 't is waar, ook geen goede stem; echter vindt men twintig goede zingers voor één goeden lezer.' Wolff and Deken, *Economische liedjes*, XXIII–XXIV.
45 Woolf, *Reading History in Early Modern England*, 82.
46 Fox, *Oral and Literate Culture in England*, 37.
47 Gasta, 'Writing to be Heard', 90.
48 Gasta, 'Señora, donde hay música', 359.
49 Richards, *Voices and Books*, Chapter 1, 'The Voice on the Page', 37–75 (quotation on 66).
50 Williams, *The Social Life of Books*, 3.
51 Cavallo and Chartier, *A History of Reading in the West*, 277: 'the practice of oralized reading that the texts describe or were designed for'.
52 Cf. Koopmans and Verhuyck, *Een kijk op anekdotencollecties*, 64.
53 'Fraeye historie ende al waer / Mach ic u tellen hoort naer / Het was op enen avontstont / Dat karel slapen begonde. [...] Hoort hier wonder ende waerhede / Wat den coninc daer ghevel / Dat weten noch die menige wel.' Duinhoven, *Karel ende Elegast*, 2r.
54 Koopmans and Verhuyck, *Een kijk op anekdotencollecties*, 76.
55 Garke, *The Use of Songs*, 65, points to the fact that songs in the early frame narratives were mostly used in the framework, rarely in the tales themselves. Later this custom would change.
56 Gasta, 'Writing to be Heard', 90 and 97, resp.
57 Chartier, 'Leisure and Sociability', 105.
58 Cervantes, *Den verstandigen vroomen ridder*, chapter 33.

8 FICTION AND REALITY

1 It is still a question of whether 'such a framework narrative [...] makes *Den Nederduytschen Helicon* a unique phenomenon in Dutch literature history', as claimed by Thijs, *De hoefslag van Pegasus*, 164.
2 'soete spelletjes te speelen, dan met diepsinnighe vraghen voor te stellen, een andermael met raetseltjes, speelen, singhen, malkander eenighe Historikens te vertellen, die wy ergens ghehoort of ghelesen hebben'. Danckertsz, *Nutte Tijdtquistingh*, 19.

3   Danckertsz, *Nutte Tijdtquistingh*, 25 et seq. This title obviously exists only within the reality of Danckertsz's novel.

4   Chaucer's *The Canterbury Tales* (c. 1400) is also a brilliant example in this category. The tales in this collection are presented as a story-telling contest by a group of pilgrims as they travel together from London to Canterbury.

5   Chartier, 'Leisure and Sociability', 104.

6   Blaak, *Geletterde levens*, 68. Cf. Moser, 'Poezijlust en vriendenliefde', 260, who points to the 'striking similarities between the fictionalised handling of literature in *Den Nederduytschen Helicon* and the actual handling of literature as evidenced by the descriptions in the diary of David Beck and the convolute manuscript of David de Moor'.

7   'Lepante, die ook met Cyllenia, en d'andere op den overloop was gekomen, hoorde Melinte deze Veerzen, die hy zo terstond gemaekt had, verhalen. En dichte op dien zelven tijd, om strijd, mede, en verhaeldenze, en daer na een Luyt vindende, voegd'er zijn stem op, en zong 'er dus.' Desmarets, *D'onvergelijkelijke Ariane*, 376–77 (the strophic form of the poem is 4 × 6 lines, and that of the song is 3 × 4 lines).

8   'Maer myn keel wort heesch, van zoo zwaren toon'. Van Hoogstraten *Haegaenveld*, 227–29.

9   E.g. Cervantes, *Den verstandigen vroomen ridder*, 304. Cf. Gasta, 'Señora, donde hay música', 363–64, for a discussion on the musicality of sonnets.

10 Elias, 'Musical Performance', 173 (note 50).

11 Larson, *The Matter of Song*, 124.

12 'om zoo wel gelezen als gezongen te konnen worden: nadien doch alle Rijm ofte gedicht, (na oudt gebruyck en oock aert van de zake) behoort soo wel leesselijck als zingelijck, en zoo wel zingelijck als leesselijck te zijn'. Camphuysen, *Stichtelycke rymen*, fol. A2r.

9 SINGING WHILE READING

1   Cf. Gasta's question cited in Chapter 7, footnote 7. However, he only speaks of oral performance in general, not of singing in particular.

2   Cf. Grootes, 'Een zeeheld op vrijersvoeten', 311. Van Gemert, 'Stenen in het mozaïek', 28: 'These texts confront the public with their own behavioural standards and make the social dimensions of literature visible.'

3   'In many cases we do not know whether the singing was accompanied or unaccompanied. Nor is it clear whether medieval reciters of oral narratives performed only alone or also in company with others.' Reichl, 'Turkic Bard and Medieval Entertainer', 168.

4   Boulton, *The Song in the Story*, 6.

5   Boulton, *The Song in the Story*, 8.

6   Boulton, *The Song in the Story*, 9.

7   Larson, *The Matter of Song*, 134.

8   Larson, *The Matter of Song*, 150.

9   On this point, see the section on Beck in Chapter 7, footnote 5.

10 'met de zoete melodie van het zingend pluimgedierte te paren, om dus God hunnen weldoener in de ruimte, dog in het eenzame, met ruym verwyderde ziele te roemen'. Quotation from the Reverend Alardus Tiele, in De Bruijn, *De hoeve en het hart*, 366.

11 'Daer ghy alleen over wegh gaet, kont ghyse by u selve soetjens ende sachtjens murmulen, het welk u den wegh niet weynigh verkorten sal, ende wesen als een aengenaam geselschap.' Sluiter, *Psalmen, lof-sangen*, XIX.

12 Quoted in Veldhorst, *Van Gogh & Music*, 30.

13 The difference is that today's novel readers are rarely confronted with new lyrics on existing tunes (contrafacts). If songs are included, it is most of the times about

existing songs, which the reader either does or does not know. In contrast, 17th-century readers could sing along with the songs, because they knew the melodies.

14 Rubery, *The Untold Story*, 15–16.

15 Van Gemert, 'Stenen in het mozaïek', 27.

16 'Beminden leser, Al hoe-wel maer by eenighe van dese Liedekens, ende niet by alle, de ghemeyne, oft wereltsche voysen ghestelt sijn, daer-se op souden connen ghesonghen worden; (t'welck gheschiet is, om datmen op alle gheene heeft connen vinden;) nochtans sullen de ghene, die gheen musieck en connen, lichtelijck de selfde vatten, hoorende die maer eens, oft tweemaels voorsinghen van de ghene die in de musieck ervaren zijn.' Van Antwerpen, *De gheestelijcke tortelduyve*, afterword.

17 Shepherd, *Continuum Encyclopedia of Popular Music*, 146. Cf. Honders, 'Psalm Singing in London', 68, who talks about several lines instead of one: 'The first lines were sung by the precentors, and then the congregation could join in by repeating the same lines.'

18 Shepherd, *Continuum Encyclopedia of Popular Music*, 147.

19 Shepherd, *Continuum Encyclopedia of Popular Music*, 147.

20 Anonymous, *Gezelschapsspelen of de kunst*, 49.

21 'Onderwijlen was Melibe en Lucretia vast besich met het boeckjen, lesende de toe-eygeningh, 't welck de Coninginne merckende, oorsaecke gaf om Constantijn, biddende, te gebieden, 't selve overluydt te willen lesen alsoo het sijn beurt was, om tot vermaeck yetwes voort te brengen: hiermee een yder plaets nemende, schicktense hun in 't ronde, Constantijn het boeckjen van Lucretia ontfangen hebbende, begon als volgt te lesen.' Danckertsz, *Nutte Tijdtquistingh*, 23.

10 CONCLUSION

1 Cf. Garke, *The Use of Songs*, 103. See also Larson, *The Matter of Song*, 125, who writes that song performance 'seems to have been associated in the period with an especially vulnerable mode of self-expression'.

2 Cf. 'emotion heavy' arias (with little text) versus the 'performative' recitation (with lots of text) in operas.

3 Cf. Garke, *The Use of Songs*, 60: 'There are three ways in which they may influence [the plot of the novel]: they may advance, suspend, or round of the action.' See also 60–63, on resp. 'promotive', 'retarding' and 'retrospective' song-insets.

4 Dubois, *Music in the Georgian Novel*, 5. His aim was 'simply to trace references to music in eighteenth-century British fiction'.

5 As aptly expressed by the media historian McLuhan, *The Gutenberg Galaxy*, 32.

6 Richards, *Voices and Books*, 14. See also 181, where she speaks of 'the need to broaden our understanding of the material book so as to recover its imagining as a "thing" that can have a life off as well as on the page'.

7 Cf. Marsh, *The Sound of Print* (English ballads on broadsides); Veldhorst, 'De vloeiendheid zoeken' (songs in Dutch poetry collections), 823; Veldhorst, *De perfecte verleiding* (songs in Dutch stage plays). Quote from Richards, *Voices and Books*, 283.

8 Mancini, 'Narrative Prose', 319.

9 'Celui-là, tout en travaillant, fredonnait en grec de petits vers d'Anacréon, qu'il accommodait à des airs à la mode.' Yourcenar, 'Un homme obscur', 105.

BIBLIOGRAPHY

Albert, Richard N. 'A Bibliography of Jazz Fiction'. *Bulletin of Bibliography* 46, 2 (1989): 129–39.

Anonymous. *Gezelschapsspelen of de kunst om zich in alle jaargetijden zoowel in de open lucht als binnenshuis aangenaam en nuttig bezig te houden.* Leiden: D. Noothoven van Goor, 1866.

Antwerpen, Gabriel van. *De gheestelijcke tortelduyve.* Antwerp: Erven P. Phalesius, 1648.

Ariosto, Ludovico. *De razende Roelant.* Amsterdam: J. J. Schipper, 1649.

Aronson, Alex. *Music and the Novel: A Study in Twentieth-Century Fiction.* Totowa: Rowman & Littlefield, 1980.

D'Audiguier, Vital. *Histoire trage-comique de nostre temps, sous les noms de Lysandre et de Caliste.* Paris: Nicolas de la Vigne, 1622.

———. *Liebes-Beschreibung Lysanders und Kalisten.* Amsterdam: Ludwig Elzevier, 1644. In Philipp von Zesen, *Sämtliche Werken* IV, 1, ed. Volker Meid. Berlin: Walter de Gruyter, 1987.

———. *A Tragi-Comicall History of our Times, under the Borrowed Names of Lisander and Calista.* London: Richard Lownes, 1652.

———. *De treurige doch bly-eyndigende historie van onsen tijdt, onder de naem van Lysander en Caliste.* Amsterdam: Baltes Boeckholt, 1663.

Bakhtin, Mikhail M. *The Dialogic Imagination.* Austin: University of Texas Press, 1981.

Balde, Johannes. *Den Lust-Hof Vande Wonderlijcke gheschiedenissen ende avontueren des Weerelts.* Rotterdam: Dirk Mullem, 1603.

Battistelli, Franco. 'Nolfi, Vincenzo'. In *Dizionario Biografico degli Italiani.* Istituto dell'Enciclopedia Italiana Treccani, 2013. http://www.treccani.it/enciclopedia/vincenzo-nolfi_(Dizionario-Biografico).

Bernhart, Walter, Steven Paul Scher and Werner Wolf (eds). *Word and Music Studies: Defining the Field. Proceedings of the First International Conference on Word and Music Studies at Graz, 1997.* Amsterdam: Rodopi, 1999.

Birken, Sigmund von. *Teutsche Rede-, Bind- und Dichtkunst: Oder, Kurze Anweisung Zur Teutschen Poesy.* Nürnberg: C. Riegel, 1679.

Blaak, Jeroen. *Geletterde levens. Dagelijks leven en schrijven in de vroegmoderne tijd in Nederland, 1624–1770.* Hilversum: Verloren, 2004.

Blasius, Joan. *Lysander en Kaliste. Bly-eyndend-Treur-spel.* Amsterdam: Jacob Lescaille, 1663.

Boekholt, Baltes. *De wonderlijke vryagien en rampzaalige, doch bly-eindige, trouw-gevallen van deze tijdt.* Amsterdam: Baltes Boekholt, 1668.

Bontekoe, W. IJ. *Journael ofte gedenckwaerdige beschrijvinghe van de Oost-Indische reijse*, ed. G. J. Hoogewerff. Utrecht: A. Oosthoek, 1915.

Boulton, Maureen Barry McCann. *The Song in the Story: Lyric Insertions in French Narrative Fiction, 1200–1400.* Philadelphia: University of Pennsylvania Press, 1993.

Boutcher, Warren. 'Transnational Cervantes: Text, Performance, and Transmission in the World of Don Quixote'. In Glomski and Moreau (eds), *Seventeenth-Century Fiction*, 99–114.

Braund, Susanna. 'Prosimetrum'. In Hubert Cancik and Helmuth Schneider (eds.). *Brill's New Pauly*. First published online in 2006. http://dx.doi.org/10.1163/1574-9347_bnp_e1010870

Brouwer, Han. 'Rondom het boek. Historisch onderzoek naar leescultuur, in het bijzonder in de achttiende eeuw. Een overzicht van bronnen en benaderingen, resultaten en problemen'. In *Documentatieblad Werkgroep Achttiende Eeuw* 20 (1988): 51–120.

Brown, K. D. *An Annotated Bibliography and Reference List of Musical Fiction*. Lewiston: Edwin Mellen Press, 2005.

Bruijn, Enny de. *De hoeve en het hart. Een boerenfamilie in de Gouden Eeuw*. Amsterdam: Prometheus, 2019.

Buisman J. Fzn., M. *Populaire prozaschrijvers van 1600 tot 1815. Romans, novellen, verhalen, levensbeschrijvingen, arcadia's, sprookjes*. Amsterdam: B. M. Israël, 1960.

Camp, Maxime du. *Souvenirs littéraires*. Tome premier. Paris: Librairie Hachette, 1892.

Camphuysen, D. R. *Stichtelycke rymen. Om te lezen of te zingen*. Hoorn: Isaac Willemsz van der Beeck, 1624.

Cavallo, Guglielmo and Chartier, Roger. *A History of Reading in the West (Studies in Print Culture and the History of the Book)*. Cambridge: Polity Press, 1999.

Cervantes y Saavedra, M. de. *Den ialoerssen Carrizale. De doorluchtige Dienstmaagd. Het schoone Heydinnetje*. Delft: Felix van Sambix, 1643.

———. *Den verstandigen vroomen ridder Don Quichot de la Mancha*. Dordrecht: Iacobus Savry, 1657.

———. *Monipodios Hol, of 't Leven, Bedrijf, en Oeffening der Gaudieven, haer onrust en schelmerijen*. Amsterdam: Evert Nieuwenhof, 1658.

———. *El zeloso estremeno: The Jealous Estremaduran: A novel*. London: D. Midwinter and B. Lintot, 1709.

———. *The Jealous Estremaduran*. London: J. Watts, 1729.

Chartier, Roger. *The Cultural Uses of Print in Early Modern France*. Princeton: Princeton University Press, 1987.

———. 'Leisure and Sociability: Reading Aloud in Early Modern Europe'. In Susan Zimmerman, Ronald F.E. Weissman (eds), *Urban Life in the Renaissance*. Newark: Associated University Presses, 1989, 103–20.

Clements, Elicia. *Virginia Woolf: Music, Sound, Language*. Toronto: University of Toronto Press, 2019.

Curtius, Ernst Robert. *European Literature and the Latin Middle Ages*. New Jersey: Princeton University Press, 1953.

Danckertsz, Cornelis. *Nutte Tijdtquistingh der Amstelsche Jonckheyt*. Amsterdam: Cornelis Danckertsz, 1640.

Desmarets, J. *D'onvergelijkelijke Ariane*. Amsterdam: J. J. Schipper, 1646.

Dubois, Pierre. *Music in the Georgian Novel*. Cambridge: Cambridge University Press, 2015.

Duinhoven, A. M. (ed.). *Karel ende Elegast. Diplomatische uitgave van de Middelnederlandse teksten en de tekst uit de Karlmeinet-compilatie*. Part 1. Zwolle: Tjeenk Willink, 1969.

Elias, Cathy Ann. 'Musical Performance in 16th-century Italian Literature. Straparola's Le piacevoli notti'. In *Early Music* 17, no: 2 (1989): 161–73.

Finkelstein, David and McCleery, Alistair. *An Introduction to Book History*. London: Routledge, 2005.

Flaherty, Gloria. 'Transport, Ecstasy, and Enthusiasm'. In Georgia Cowart (ed.), *French Musical Thought, 1600–1800*, 81–93. Ann Arbor: UMI Research Press, 1989.

Fox, Adam. *Oral and Literate Culture in England, 1500–1700*. Oxford: Clarendon Press, 2000.

Freedman, William. *Laurence Sterne and the Origins of the Musical Novel*. Athens: University of Georgia Press, 1978.

Frow, John. *Genre (The New Critical Idiom)*. London: Routledge, 2015.

Fuller, Thomas. *Andronicus, of Rampsalige Arghlistigheyt*. Amsterdam: Joost Pluymer, 1659.

Garke, Esther C. *The Use of Songs in Elizabethan Prose Fiction*. Bern: Francke, 1972.

Gasta, Chad M. ' "Señora, donde hay música no puede haber cosa mala." Music, Poetry, and Orality in "Don Quijote" '. In *Hispania* 93, no. 3 (2010): 357–67.

———. 'Writing to be Heard: Performing Music in Don Quixote'. In Julia Domínguez (ed.), *Cervantes in Perspective*, 87–109. World Languages and Cultures Publications 32. Madrid: Iberoamericana, 2013.

Gemert, Lia van. 'Stenen in het mozaïek: de vroegmoderne Nederlandse roman als internationaal fenomeen'. In *Tijdschrift voor Nederlandse Taal- en Letterkunde* 124, no: 1 (2008): 20–30.

Gibbs, John R. *Music Fiction / Music in Literature: A Bibliography of Musical Fiction*. Washington: University of Washington, 2016.

Glomski, Jacqueline and Moreau, Isabelle (eds). *Seventeenth-Century Fiction: Text and Transmission*. Oxford: Oxford University Press, 2016.

Godwin, Francis. *Het rechte eerste Deel van de Man in de Maen, ofte een Verhael van een Reyse derwaerts gedaen door Domingo Gonzales, de spoedige Bode*. Amsterdam: Jacob Benjamin, 1651.

Godwin, Francis. *The Man in the Moone*. Ed. William Poole. Ontario: Broadview Press, 2009.

Griffith, Karlyn. 'Performative Reading and Receiving a Performance of the Jour du Jugement in MS Besançon 579'. In *Comparative Drama* 45, no: 2 (2011): 99–126

Grootes, E. K. 'Een zeeheld op vrijersvoeten. Hoe Cornelis Tromp figureert in een roman uit 1668, over de plaats van dit werk in de romantraditie en over het beoogde leespubliek'. In *De Zeventiende Eeuw* 20, no: 2 (2004): 305–21.

Hart, Thomas H. *Cervantes' Exemplary Fictions. A Study of the Novelas Ejemplares*. Lexington: University Press of Kentucky, 1993.

Heinsius, Nicolaas. *Don Clarazel de Gontarnos, ofte den buyten-spoorigen dolenden ridder*. Amsterdam: Nathaniel Holbeek and Johannes Broers, 1697.

Heliodorus. *De getrouwe liefde van de kuysche Theagenes en de zuyvere Cariclea*. Amsterdam: Ian van Duisberg, 1659.

Hocutt, Daniel H. 'Music and Rhetoric in *Tristram Shandy*. Challenging Eighteenth-Century Rational Intellectualism'. In R. Hilliard, *Special Topics in Comedy and Satire in Eighteenth Century Literature*, 1–21. Richmond: University of Richmond, 1997.

Homerus. *De Dooling van Ulisses. In vierentwintig Boeken*, vert. G. van Staveren. Amsterdam: Gerrit van Goedesberg and Klaas Fransz, 1651.

Honders, A. C. 'Psalm Singing in London, 1550–1553'. In *IAH-Bulletin* 9 (1981): 64–69.

Hooft, P. C. *Granida*. Ed. Lia van Gemert. Amsterdam: Amsterdam University Press, 1998.

Hoogstraten, Samuel van. *Schone Rooseliin of De getrouwe liefde van Panthus*. Dordrecht: Jasper Gorisz., 1650.

———. *De gestrafte ontschaking of zeeghafte herstelling van den iongen Haegaenveld*. Amsterdam: Baltus Boekholt, 1669.

Ionescu, Christina (ed.). *Book Illustration in the Long Eighteenth Century. Reconfiguring the Visual Periphery of the Text*. Newcastle upon Tyne: Cambridge Scholars Publishing, 2011.

Jansen, Jeroen. 'Johan de Brune en de stijldeugden'. In Verkruijsse, P.J. (ed.), *Johan de Brune de Oude (1588–1658). Een Zeeuws literator en staatsman uit de zeventiende eeuw*, 70–91. Middelburg: Koninklijk Zeeuwsch Genootschap der Wetenschappen, 1990.

Keymer, Martin. *Prose Fiction in English from the Origins of Print to 1750. The Oxford History of the Novel in English. Volume 1*. Oxford: Oxford University Press, 2017.

Koopmans, Jelle and Verhuyck, Paul. *Een kijk op anekdotencollecties in de zeventiende eeuw. Jan Zoet, Het leven en bedrijf van Clément Marot*. Amsterdam: Rodopi, 1991.

Koppenol, Johan. 'Zoveel jeu en toch niet te lezen. Romans uit de zeventiende eeuw'. In *De Groene Amsterdammer. Literatuur* 130, no. 1 (2006): 42–45.

Kundera, Milan. *The Art of the Novel*. New York: Grove Press, 1986.

———. *Testaments Betrayed. An Essay in Nine Parts*. New York: HarperCollins, 1993.

Lankhorst, Otto S. 'Lezen onder het eten. Voorlezen in kloosterrefters'. In Anrooij, W. van and Hoftijzer, P. (eds), *Lezen in de Lage Landen. Studies over tien eeuwen leescultuur*, 219–24. Hilversum: Verloren, 2017.

Larson, Katherine. *The Matter of Song in Early Modern England: Texts in and of the Air*. Oxford: Oxford University Press, 2019.

Leemans, Inger. *Het woord is aan de onderkant: radicale ideeën in Nederlandse pornografische romans, 1670–1700*. Nijmegen: Vantilt, 2002.

Les nouvelles de Miquel de Cervantes Saavedra. Traduictes d'Espagnol en Français: les six premiers par F. de Rosset. Et les autres six par Sr. D'Audiguier. Paris: Jean Richer, 1615.

Mancini, Albert N. 'Narrative Prose'. In Peter Brand and Lino Pertile (eds), *The Cambridge History of Italian Literature*, 318–35. Cambridge: Cambridge University Press, 1996.

Manguel, Alberto. *A History of Reading*. London: Harper Collins, 1996.

Marsh, Christopher. *Music and Society in Early Modern England*. Cambridge: Cambridge University Press, 2010.

Marsh, Christopher. 'The Sound of Print in Early Modern England: the Broadside Ballad as Song'. In Julia Crick and Alexandra Walsham (eds), *The Uses of Script and Print, 1300–1700*, 171–90. Cambridge: Cambridge University Press, 2004.

Martin, Christophe. 'L'Illustration de *L'Astrée* (XVIIe–XVIIIe siècles)'. In Denis, Delphine (ed.), *Lire L'Astrée*, 203–39. Paris: Presses Universitaire de Paris-Sorbonne, 2008.

McLuhan, Marshall. *The Gutenberg Galaxy. The Making of Typographic Man*. Toronto: University of Toronto Press, 1962.

Moore, Steven. *The Novel. An Alternative History, 1600–1800*. New York: Bloomsbury, 2013.

Moreau, Isabelle. 'Seventeenth-Century Fiction in the Making'. In Glomski and Moreau, *Seventeenth-Century Fiction*, 1–16.

Moser, Nelleke. 'Overdroomde dromen. Haring van Harinxma (1604–1669) als vertaler van Quevedo's Sueños'. In *Jaarboek voor Nederlandse boekgeschiedenis* 9 (2002): 41–56. Leiden: Nederlandse Boekhistorische Vereniging.

———. '"Poezijlust en vriendenliefde." Literaire sociabiliteit in handschrift en druk na 1600'. In *Spiegel der Letteren* 49, no. 2 (2007): 247–64.

Noske, Frits. 'Sound and Sentiment. The Function of Music in the Gothic Novel'. In *Music and Letters* 62, no. 2 (1981): 162–66.

Omeis, Magnus Daniel. *Gründliche Anleitung zur Teutschen accuraten Reim- und Dichtkunst*. Vol. 1. Nürnberg: Michahelles und Adolph, 1704.

Packham, J. 'Pip's Oceanic Voice. Speech and the Sea in Moby-Dick'. In *The Modern Language Review* 112, no: 3 (2017): 567–84.

Pavel, Thomas G. *The Lives of the Novel: A History*. New Jersey: Princeton University Press, 2013.

Petermann, Emily. *The Musical Novel. Imitation of Musical Structure, Performance, and Reception in Contemporary Fiction*. Rochester: Camden House, 2014.

Pol, L. R. *Romanbeschouwing in voorredes. Een onderzoek naar het denken over de roman in Nederland tussen 1600 en 1755*. Part 1: Study. Utrecht: HES Uitgevers, 1987.

Porteman, Karel. ' "J'ay pris pour duppes tous les Pays-Bas." Jean Puget de la Serre en de Nederlanden'. In J. Andriessen, A. Keersmakers, P. Lenders (eds), *Cultuurgeschiedenis in de Nederlanden van de Renaissance naar de Romantiek*, 217–38. Leuven/Amersfoort: Acco, 1986.

Porteman, Karel and Smits-Veldt, Mieke B. *Een nieuw vaderland voor de muzen. Geschiedenis van de Nederlandse literatuur, 1560–1700*. Amsterdam: Bert Bakker, 2008.

Quevedo, F. de. *Seven wonderlijcke ghesichten*. Leeuwarden: Dirck Albertsz, 1641.

Reichl, Karl. 'Turkic Bard and Medieval Entertainer. What a Living Epic Tradition can tell us about Oral Performance of Narrative in the Middle Ages'. In Vitz, Regalado and Lawrence, *Performing Medieval Narrative*, 167–78.

Richards, Jennifer. *Voices & Books in the English Renaissance. A New History of Reading*. Oxford: Oxford University Press, 2019.

Rippl, Gabriele (ed.). *Handbook of Intermediality. Literature – Image – Sound – Music*. Handbooks of English and American Studies 1. Berlin: De Gruyter, 2015.

Rooy, Piet de. *Een geschiedenis van het onderwijs in Nederland*. Amsterdam: Wereldbibliotheek, 2018.

Rosset, F. de. *Waerachtige treurige gheschiedenissen onzes tijdts*. Amsterdam: Broer Iansz., 1632.

Rubery, Matthew. *The Untold Story of the Talking Book*. Cambridge, MA: Harvard University Press, 2016.

Ryan, Judith. 'Hybrid Forms in German Romanticism'. In Harris, J. and Reichl, K. (eds), *Prosimetrum. Crosscultural Perspectives on Narrative in Prose and Verse*, 165–81. Cambridge: D.S. Brewer, 1997.

Schlegel, Friedrich. *Gespräch über die Poesie*. Nachwort Hans Eichner. Stuttgart: J.B. Metzler, 1968.

Sels, Willem Hendrik. *Zedelyke uitspanningen, bestaande in vier geschiedenissen. Met konstplaaten. Eerste deel*. Amsterdam: F. de Kruyff, 1771.

Seters, W. H. van. 'De Nederlandse uitgaven van *The Man in the Moone*'. In *Het Boek* 31, no. 3 (1953): 157–72.

Shepherd, John. *Continuum Encyclopedia of Popular Music of the World*, II: Performance and Production, vol. 11. London: A&C Black, 2003.

Sluiter, Willem. *Psalmen, lof-sangen, ende geestelike liedekens*. Deventer: Jan Colom 1661.

Smyth, Gerry. *Music in Contemporary British Fiction. Listening to the Novel*. Basingstoke: Palgrave Macmillan, 2008

Solbach, Andreas. 'Early Modern German Narrative Prose'. In Max Reinhart (ed.), *Early Modern German Literature, 1350–1700*. Camden House History of German Literature, vol. 4. New York: Camden House, 2007.

Spies, Marijke and Frijhoff, Willem T. M. *Hard-Won Unity. Dutch Culture in a European Perspective*. Groningen/Basingstoke: Royal van Gorcum/Palgrave Macmillan, 2004.

Tasso, Torquato. *Het Verloste Jeruzalem*. Rotterdam: Joannes Naeranus, 1658.

Thijs, Boukje. *De hoefslag van Pegasus. Een cultuurhistorisch onderzoek naar Den Nederduytschen Helicon (1610)*. Hilversum: Verloren, 2004.

Thomas, Downing A. *Music and the Origins of Language. Theories from the French Enlightenment*. Cambridge: Cambridge University Press, 1995.

Tucker, Holly. ' "Une autre de vostre ventre." Parodie Musicality in Charles Sorel's Histoire comique de Francion and Le Berger extravagant'. *French Forum* 24, no. 3 (1999): 303–14.

Veldhorst, Natascha. *De perfecte verleiding. Muzikale scènes op het Amsterdams toneel in de zeventiende eeuw*. Amsterdam: Amsterdam University Press, 2004.

———. 'Musical Life'. In Spies and Frijhoff, *Hard-Won Unity*, 584–94.

———. 'Pharmacy for the Body and Soul. Dutch Songbooks in the Seventeenth Century'. In *Early Music History* 27 (2008): 217–86.

———. 'Vergilius' Bucolica op muziek. Focquenbroch en de Hollandse liedcultuur'. In *Fumus. Mededelingen van de stichting Willem Godschalck van Focquenbroch* 7 (2009): 31–36.

———. *Zingend door het leven. Het Nederlandse liedboek in de Gouden Eeuw*. Amsterdam: Amsterdam University Press, 2009.

———. *Van Gogh & Music. Symphony in Blue and Yellow*. New Haven: Yale University Press, 2018.

———. ' "De vloeiendheid zoeken met het oordeel der oren." Hooft en de muziek'. In Johan Koppenol, Ton van Strien and Natascha Veldhorst (eds), *P. C. Hooft. De gedichten*, 823–49. Amsterdam: Athenaeum-Polak & Van Gennep 2012.

Vitz, Evelyn Birge. *Orality and Performance in Early French Romance*. Woodbridge: Boydell & Brewer, 1999.

Vitz, Evelyn Birge, Nancy Freeman Regalado and Marilyn Lawrence (eds). *Performing Medieval Narrative*. Cambridge: D.S. Brewer, 2005.

Vogler, Frederick Wright. *Vital d'Audiguier and the Early Seventeenth-Century French Novel*. Chapel Hill: University of North Carolina Press, 1964.

Watt, Ian. *The Rise of the Novel. Studies in Defoe, Richardson and Fielding*. Berkeley: University of California Press, 1965.

Weduwen, Arthur der. 'The Politics of Print in the Dutch Golden Age: The Ommelander Troubles (c. 1630–1680)'. In Nina Lamal, Jamie Cumby, Helmer J. Helmers (eds), *Print and Power in Early Modern Europe (1500–1800)*, 148–77. Leiden: Brill, 2021.

Williams, Abigail. *The Social Life of Books. Reading Together in the Eighteenth-Century Home*. New Haven: Yale University Press, 2017.

Winkel, Jan te. *De ontwikkelingsgang der Nederlandsche letterkunde IV. Geschiedenis der Nederlandsche letterkunde van de Republiek der Vereenigde Nederlanden (2)*. Haarlem: De erven F. Bohn, 1924.

Weststeijn, Thijs. 'Samuel van Hoogstraten: the First Dutch Novelist?' In Thijs Weststeijn (ed.), *The Universal Art of Samuel van Hoogstraten (1627–1678): Painter, Writer, Courtier*, 183–207. Amsterdam: Amsterdam University Press, 2013.

Wolf, Werner. *The Musicalization of Fiction. A Study in the Theory and History of Intermediality*. Amsterdam: Rodopi, 1999.

———. 'Musicalized Fiction and Intermediality. Theoretical Aspects of Word and Music Studies'. In Bernhart, Scher and Wolf, *Word and Music Studies*, 38–58.

———. 'Literature and Music: Theory'. In Rippl, *Handbook of Intermediality*, 459–74.

Worp, J. A. *Briefwisseling van Constantijn Huygens. Section 2: 1634–1639*. The Hague: Martinus Nijhoff, 1911.

Woolf, Virginia. 'The Countess of Pembroke's Arcadia'. In Virginia Woolf, *The Common Reader*. Second Series. 3rd ed. London: Hogarth Press, 1945, 40–50.

Woolf, Daniel R. *Reading History in Early Modern England*. Cambridge Studies in Early Modern British History. Cambridge: Cambridge University Press, 2000.

Wolff, Betje and Deken, Aagje. *Economische liedjes*. The Hague: Isaac van Cleef, 1781.

Yourcenar, Marguerite. 'Un homme obscur'. In Marguerite Yourcenar, *Comme l'eau qui coule*, 77–206. Paris: Editions Gallimard, 1982.

INDEX